Marmont on Warfare

AUG.ᵗᵉ FRED.ᶜ LOUIS VIESSE DE MARMONT,
Duc de Raguse   Maréchal et Pair de France
Major Général de   la Garde Royale
Né a Chatillon sur Seine   le 20 Juillet 1774.

Marmont on Warfare

An Appraisal of the Military Art by One of
Napoleon's Marshals with a Biography
of the Author

On Modern Armies

Auguste de Marmont

Auguste de Marmont, Duke of Ragusa (Extract)

R. P. Dunn-Pattison

LEONAUR

Marmont on Warfare
An Appraisal of the Military Art by One of Napoleon's Marshals with a
Biography of the Author
On Modern Armies
by Auguste de Marmont
Auguste de Marmont, Duke of Ragusa
by R. P. Dunn-Pattison

FIRST EDITION

First published under the titles
On Modern Armies
and
Auguste de Marmont, Duke of Ragusa (Extract)

Leonaur is an imprint of Oakpast Ltd

Copyright in this form © 2014 Oakpast Ltd

ISBN: 978-1-78282-265-3 (hardcover)
ISBN: 978-1-78282-266-0 (softcover)

http://www.leonaur.com

Publisher's Notes

The views expressed in this book are not necessarily
those of the publisher.

Contents

Preface of the Translator

The reputation of Marshal Marmont is too well established to call for any comment. Fifty years' service and twenty campaigns, either as lieutenant of Napoleon or as commander-in-chief, give great authority to his opinions on military matters.

This work, from which many writers have largely borrowed, is, in itself, a treatise of the military art, and it has the great merit of being interesting while treating of professional matters.

To those officers who are not familiar with French, an English version will be acceptable; indeed, I always thought so, for this translation was made six years ago. When, lately, Mr. Mitchell observed that officers regretted the absence of an original treatise of modern date which might used as a standard, I brought him this manuscript.

Making an exception for the chapter on artillery, which is out of date, I introduce Marmont to the Non-French readers as the best work we have on modern armies.

The title differs from the original, *Esprit des Institutions Militaires*. While conveying an exact idea of the contents of the text, it turns the difficulty of rendering French words which have no equivalent value in English.

A. F. Lendy.

June, 1865,
Sunbury.

Introduction

None of the modern works on the military art or institutions contains a complete treatise on the subject. Some special essays on the different arms have been published, but, in general, no attempt has been made in these to establish the principles of the matter. We find in them superficial views, technical and minute details, without any sufficient indication of the end and the means.

Ancient writers went more deeply into military questions; but of what value can their theories be now, since the discovery of gunpowder has so completely revolutionised the art of war?

We may still look into Polybius and Vegetius to satisfy our curiosity, but it would be vain to search their writings for useful and applicable instruction.

The ancient and the modern wars have no resemblance to one another, unless it be in their moral aspect, or that sublime part of the art that consists in the knowledge of the human, heart—a knowledge so important at all times for the guidance of men, and which, in war, exercises a still more prompt and decisive influence.

Everything is changed in the form and in the proportion of the weapons used; their greater range keeps the combatants at greater distances from one another, they inspire more terror, and they also produce prodigious material results.

Let us add, that in former times the combatants were less numerous.

The command now-a-days is beset with more difficulties than formerly. Among the ancients, who always fought hand to hand, the army was arranged in a compact form; the small number of combatants occupied a very limited space, their front scarcely equalling that of one of our brigades. A general could see every one of his soldiers, or at least be seen by all of them. With his operations on such a small scale, the supreme chief could be everywhere present; and he was himself a combatant, setting the example sword in hand. Now-a-days the general fights with his mind and his will; it is unimportant whether he is master or not of the sword exercise; his menial eye embraces a much larger sphere of vision than his physical eye can see. In a word, a general is much less of a soldier, though he is occasionally obliged to be one, than a moral being who, by his influence over the minds of others, seems to govern events like the mysterious powers of nature.

Thus modern warfare is quite a new art, which can derive no lesson and no model from the wars of the Greeks and Romans.

If the greatest captains of antiquity, such as Alexander, Hannibal, or Caesar, were to return to this world and find themselves in a field of battle, their genius would understand nothing of what were going on; and they would require to go through more than one campaign in order to apprehend thoroughly the mechanism of the business, the consequences of our institutions and new weapons.

These truths are so evident to all who have been engaged in war, that we are at a loss to comprehend how, in the time of Louis XIV., the reveries of Chevalier Follard, and, subsequently, the still more absurd reveries of M. Menil Durand, could have been treated so seriously as to lead to the establishment (at Bayeux) of a camp, expressly for the purpose of making comparative experiments in formations and manoeuvres.

ut even more surprising is it, that a general of our own times, (Rogniat, General of the Engineers' Corps), an officer of distinction in his own special branch, should have written a large book, in which these mental aberrations are resuscitated and amplified; and yet he must at least have witnessed some battles, though he may not have figured as an actual combatant

What I have endeavoured to do is, to give, within restricted limits, an account of the spirit of military operations, organisation, and institutions. I have sought to demonstrate that nothing ought to be left to chance in these matters, that everything connected with them ought to depend on a generative principle whence the necessary consequences should flow.

A principle is discovered by considering well the end to be arrived at, and then seeking the best mode of attaining that end. The principles being found, genius makes the application of them; in this consists the whole art of war.

It has appeared to me most useful to expose them in the simplest

10

possible manner, and to construct, as it were, the rudiments of the military art, embracing at once all the branches of that art and the different services of the army, avoiding all technical quackery, with which such instruction is too often associated.

The studies of military men should not be limited to these principles; they ought also to read attentively the history of the campaigns of the great generals; for all the genius of those superior men consists in the application of the principles to practice.

In this respect our military literature is very rich, but a selection is advisable. We should by preference go to the source; we should study only the works of those who have commanded, for there is small advantage to be expected from the accounts of campaigns narrated by subaltern officers, who, ignorant of all the difficulties of the command and often of the very rudiments of the art, assume the airs of masters and the vocation of censors; Thersits-like, they are bitter in their language but faint at heart and feeble of arm, more fit to prate than to fight. Their works are a tissue of errors and falsehoods.

At the head of all the documents that deserve thorough study I should recommend the writings dictated by Napoleon and published under the title of *Memoirs of Montholon*. Every line teems with superior genius, powerful reasoning, and the authority of the great captain. His judgments and his explanations, though sometimes open to controversy, are pregnant with instruction; he who can study and apprehend them aright, must have the instinct of war.

An older work which cannot be too attentively perused is the book published by Archduke Charles of Austria, under the title of *Principles of Strategy*. We there see the application of his principles to the movements executed by him in 1796 against the armies of the Rhine and Sambre-et-Meuse; it is a *picture* of all the rules of high military art.

The memoirs of Marshal Gouvion-St.-Cyr and the history of the Russian campaign by M. de Segur[1] may also be read with profit. From such sources we may derive much instruction and accurate notions.

I have long devoted my attention to the constitution of the different arms and their best employment, and I believe the principles I am about to lay down to be true. I recommend them to those ardent,

---

1. In 1826, I spent a whole day inspecting the field of Battle of Borodino, accompanied by several French and Russian officers who had been present at the battle; I read on the ground the three well-known narrations of Segur, Chambray and Boutourlin; in my judgment the first mentioned is the only one that gives an accurate account of the mode in which the various incidents must have occurred.

intelligent and valorous youths who have stepped into our places; for them I have written the following pages.

The work I now publish is the last contribution I am able, at the end of my life, to offer for the promotion of a science I have always cultivated with ardour, and of a profession I have always followed with enthusiasms

I have experienced a real pleasure in devoting my leisure hours to this *résumé* of my studies and recollections. It is besides the fruits of meditations developed in my mind by very long and frequent conversations with Napoleon, by twenty campaigns and by half a century of experience.

CHAPTER 1

Definitions

Before entering on my subject, I shall commence by a few definitions.

The art of war is the totality of the knowledge necessary in order to lead a mass of armed men, to organise it, to move it, to make it fight, and to give to its component elements their greatest value while providing for their conservation.

The genius of war consists in the talent of applying this knowledge where it is needed, and of resorting to the best combinations with certainty and promptitude, in the midst of dangers and catastrophes.

The genius of war is incomplete in a general, unless, to the faculty of combinations which I may term technical, he adds a knowledge of the human heart, an instinct for divining what is passing through the minds of his soldiers, and of the enemy. Such inspirations, which differ so much in different persons, constitute the moral aspect of war; a mysterious action which gives a momentary power to an army, making one man equal to ten, and ten men not worth one.

There are two other faculties equally necessary—authority and decision; these are gifts of nature.

But if a great general requires a large amount of intelligence, he needs still more character. It is character that presides over the execution. In both ancient and modern times it has given their lustre to the foremost order of generals.

The military arts consist of a knowledge of the scientific or mechanical processes which regulate the details of action, or the employment of means.

Thus strategy, tactics, artillery, fortification, the organisation and administration of armies, are military arts with which a general should be familiar. Each art has its theory; but the faculty of making advantageous employment of it is only to be obtained by frequent use and the spirit of observation.

Of all human events, those relating to war do unquestionably demand most the co-operation of that auxiliary termed "experience." We must accustom ourselves to dangers, to that feature of battles which presents so many different phenomena. A man naturally brave may be able from the first to expose himself to danger without fear or suffering of any kind, sometimes with a feeling of pleasure even, but time alone can confer on him the faculty of judging how he may make the most useful sacrifice of his life.

Finally, the *profession of arms* is a consecration of one's life to military labours: and this expression is more particularly applicable to those to whom the execution is committed.

CHAPTER 2

General Principles

The general principles for the conduct of armies are not numerous, but in their application a number of combinations arise which it
is impossible to foresee and to enumerate as rules.

The conditions in which an army may find itself placed vary infinitely: the principal points of view are—the *ensemble* of the elements
composing it; the relative state of the two armies; the nature of the
seat of the war and of the neighbouring countries; the part we have
to play, whether offensive or defensive; the reputation, the character of
the general opposed to us, &c., &c.

These different circumstances open an immense field for combinations; the most comprehensive mind will fail to embrace them
all. Hence the greatest generals commit mistakes, the best are those
who make the fewest. The greater the number of *elements* we admit
into our calculations, the more command shall we have over the issue; foresight should embrace the possible as well as the probable; we
should provide even against accidental risks. It is thus that in the day
of defeat great catastrophes are obviated.

This kind of foresight was one of Napoleon's highest faculties in
his best time; his adversaries being almost always destitute of it, the
results he obtained astonished the world.

I shall establish as principles some rules which a general ought
never to lose sight of. I shall indicate the end to be obtained; but the
means are always subordinate to circumstances.

If two armies be of nearly the same numerical force and in the
same moral state, the chances are equal. In order to render them more
favourable we should so combine our movements as to deceive the
enemy, and by exciting his fears induce him to divide his forces. Then
the ablest general, suddenly concentrating his own forces, overwhelms

his adversary; and the momentary superiority he has acquired, renders his victory all the more easy.

Numerical superiority during an actual engagement is of extreme importance. No doubt the quality ranks before the quantity of the troops, but in the present state of the European armies, the number and the combination of the means contribute powerfully to success.

It is otherwise when we are opposed to barbarians who, destitute of instruction and discipline, do not form a compact aggregation; operating without skill and harmony they are always inferior in a given time to the weaker but well-combined mass opposed to them. Two successive ineffectual attacks, often one only, suffice to induce the most cowardly among them to decamp; the contagion of example seizes upon the rest and soon they all run away. In that case opinion supplies the place of arms. Thus are explained the wars of the Greeks with the Persians, the battles of Marathon and of Platea, the conquests of Alexander, the triumphs of the small Roman armies over the Germans and the Gauls, and in our own days the successes of European armies against the Turks, in spite of the disproportion of numbers.

With the view of dispersing the forces of the enemy, we must harass him, particularly upon the points necessary for his security, and we must seize with promptitude upon the moment when he yields to appearance, to attack him on a weak point with superior forces. This is precisely what would be called, in fencing terms, a feint, in a sword fight between two individuals. Two or three partial advantages prepare the way for more complete ones, which decide the fate of the campaign.

From this we see how important it is for a general to assume the initiative in the movements; we thus secure a command over the mind of our adversary, and a first success often gives us an ascendancy which we never afterwards lose. But we must watch for the favourable moment. Too great a disproportion in the forces and the different means would be an insurmountable obstacle; we should wait until the confidence of the enemy has led him to commit some faults. Promptly seizing the opportunity, an able general may obtain an advantage which shall enable him to reverse the parts hitherto played by each respectively, and to pass from the defensive to the offensive.

This is precisely what happened in 1796, in the immortal Italian campaign. The French Army, on its arrival at the frontiers of the Tyrol, was on the defensive, and found itself greatly inferior to the Austrian Army, augmented by the reinforcements which Wurmser had brought up in person. The enemy's general in his attack had divided his forces; the French general united his, and soon a first success enabled him to assume the offensive in his turn. Thence a series of victories, in combats where the French Army was almost always superior in numbers on the field of battle. To resume, in one word, that part of the art of war which applies to the general movements of armies, we should say that it is always founded on a calculation of time, of distance, and of rapidity.

CHAPTER 3

Of the Bases and Lines of Operation and of Strategy

The *base of operations* of an army consists in the country it covers, which provides for its necessities, which sends it every day all the articles it consumes, as men, horses, food, and ammunition, which receives its sick and wounded, &c.

The line of operations is determined by the general direction of the march, which is indicated by the object of operations or the point to be attained.

The general movements which are executed out of sight of the enemy, and before the battle, are called *strategy*.

Strategical points are those which it is important to occupy, either in order to menace the enemy's communications, or to cover our own. They should be chosen so as to facilitate the combinations of movements of the different columns of an army. In general, a place where many roads meet is a strategical point; in a mountainous district, the place where several villages unite is a strategical point.

Strategical lines are those which unite various strategical points which serve for the movements executed among them; they should be as short as possible.

The judicious choice of strategical points and lines is the salvation of armies in the case of defeats and the cause of the greatest results in the case of successes.

Napoleon had, in a peculiar degree, the genius of strategy; no general ever surpassed him in that respect; no one ever understood better than he how to select, beforehand, the points where he ought to strike.

A large army is composed of several columns; they are necessarily separated in order that they may live and move easily. The most distant parts ought to be able to arrive in time for the battle, whether they are to take part in the fight or only to act as a reserve. The object of strategy is to arrange the march for the most rapid concentration upon the same point, which may be at one time the centre, at another, one of the wings. A march arranged in this manner is what Napoleon used to call his chessboard.

All his first campaigns had this character, except at Marengo, when he departed from this principle, and was at the point of being beaten; on the day of action he was always seen to assemble on the field of battle all the forces he could reasonably dispose of.

Moreau, on the contrary, whose talents have been so highly vaunted, knew nothing about strategy—his ability lay in tactics. Personally very brave, he manoeuvred well in presence of the enemy the troops within his immediate view; but he fought his principal battles with only a portion of his forces.

At Hohenlinden, where his success was so brilliant, Moreau ought to have been defeated, and this he would in all probability have been had not the Austrians manoeuvred with unexampled carelessness. The French army was composed of twelve divisions; the three on the right, commanded by General Lecourbe, and the three on the left, under General Sainte-Suzanne, took no part in the battle. The Austrian Army was united, but disordered in its march; the central column, which met with no obstacle, and followed the high road with almost all the artillery, presented itself alone, and without being formed; it could thus be attacked in flank. This piece of good fortune was not owing to Moreau's dispositions. General Richepanse, a man of ability and courage, finding his division surrounded by the Austrian troops, which were beginning to organise themselves, showed front in every direction, and took one hundred pieces of artillery which were marching in column along the road.

The re-union of an army when the battle begins being the end, and rapidity in marching the means, the divisions, which are the separate units, ought to combine, and, in order to do so, they must be very moveable. Under any circumstance an army can march but slowly, but rapidity may be given to its component elements. Hence it will be well not to overload the artillery and commissariat departments. I do not approve of the custom the Russians have of encumbering themselves with guns. The grand reserves of materials and all sorts of provisions ought to march independently, to be able to protect themselves, and, in case of necessity, to be escorted by special troops. The general commanding should take care to keep them always within reach of the place where they may be most usefully employed, according as they are wanted.

Another object that should occupy the attention of the general is to protect completely his line of operation, while, at the same time, he threatens that of the enemy. Free communications are essential for the maintenance of an army; once these are lost, its moral state is imperilled. Confidence, which is the power of opinion, and for which there is no substitute in an army, cannot always withstand such a trial

Thence the necessity for a large base of operation. It is highly advantageous, if on this base there are a fortified place and several fortified points, or if a river proves part of it. The more extensive this base, the better is the line of operations covered. This was a fundamental axiom of Napoleon's; he never departed from it with impunity. In his masterly campaigns of 1806, 1806 and 1809, he gave splendid examples of it, and he made able use of the favourable circumstances that afforded him the direction of our frontier.

Two armies which have parallel bases of operation of the same extent are in similar conditions, and if one of them turns the other, it is perforce turned itself; but it is otherwise if the two bases of operation are of different lengths, or inclined towards each other. In 1805, the French Army, after a fine march from the coasts of the channel to Germany, advanced upon the flank or rear of the Austrian Army, which had invaded Bavaria—a battle lost on the Danube would have thrown it back to the Rhine, a battle gained made the vanquished army lay down its arms.

In 1806, the French Army, at the commencement of the campaign, found itself on the flank of the Prussian Army: it still maintained its communications free with France from Mentz to Basel; and these communications were so well preserved that a defeat could not do much harm, and a single victory brought the results—which are now well known.

In 1812, when Napoleon removed too far from his point of departure (for it ought to be noticed that the dimensions of a base of operation, to fulfil its requirements, are not absolute, but relative to the line of operation), his base disappeared. Established at first on the position of various bodies of troops, it would have sufficed had the army remained nearer the frontier. But these bodies being abandoned to themselves, being moveable, exposed to the chances of war, and encountering bodies of the enemy at least their equal in strength, the army in the end lost all its communications. Arrived at the banks of the Beresina, Napoleon was necessarily beaten, and the remains of his army would have been utterly annihilated, had it not been for a kind of miracle, of which Admiral Tschitschagoff and General Kaptzievitsch may take the merit.

But there are circumstances in which it is useful to change the direction of our line of operation in the very middle of a campaign, and to select another base; and although the most natural idea and the usual custom is to place ourselves in front of the country we wish to defend, it sometimes happens that we may give security more efficaciously by taking a line of operation which seems to abandon and deliver it over to the enemy.

In 1797, after the capitulation of Mantua, when the French Army marched on Vienna, the Austrian Army, which found itself too weak to offer battle, retreated in the' direction of the capital. If in place of doing this it had posted itself in the Tyrol, the natural obstacles of that country would have established a sort of equilibrium between the respective forces; the newly-levied troops from Hungary and Croatia, which could be of no use in battle, would have sufficed to cover the Friouli frontier, keep a body of French troops in check, and paralyse its action, in spite of the excellence of its soldiers (for the French Army had none but such soldiers).

Again, if the Austrian Army had taken that line of operation, it would have intercepted the reinforcements, which could only have come to the French Army from the Rhine. Lastly, if the war had brought the belligerent armies into Suabia and Bavaria, all the Austrian forces, reunited at the centre of the operations, would have been enabled to manoeuvre under the most advantageous conditions. Therefore the Austrian army did very wrong in taking the line of operation it adopted.

Here is another example:—In 1814 the Marshal Duke of Dalmatia (Soult), after having operated on the Adour, was obliged to quit the basin of that river, and he took his line of operation on Toulouse. In that he acted wisely, for thereby he drew off the English Army from the centre of France more certainly than if he had retreated upon Bordeaux, whither it would have followed him; a small body of troops, supported by National Guards placed behind the *landes* and covering Bordeaux, would have ensured the safety of that town, had not the spirit of the time and the political complications rendered these wise dispositions useless.

To resume, strategy has a twofold purpose:—

1st. To reunite all our troops, or the greatest possible number, on the spot where the battle is to be fought, when the enemy can only muster a portion of his; in other words, to secure a numerical superiority of numbers for the day of battle.

2nd. To cover and secure our own communications, while we threaten those of the enemy.

CHAPTER 4

On Tactics

Tactics is the art of handling troops on a field of battle and of making them march without confusion. What is to be done is to maintain order in the midst of the apparent disorder produced by this multitude of men, horses and machines, which together compose an army, and to gain the greatest possible advantages from it.

Tactics is the. science of the application of manoeuvre: one may be a great manoeuvre without possessing a particle of genius, but not without great practice: nothing is easier to understand than the theory, but the practice is not without difficulties. The general must be familiar with the means foreseen and calculated by the regulations, he must at a glance know how to judge of the ground, to calculate distances, to determine directions precisely, to appreciate details, and to combine the chain of circumstances.

This kind of merit was incomplete in Napoleon, which is explained by the first part of his career.

A simple officer of artillery until the moment when he became the head of armies, he had never commanded a regiment, nor a brigade, nor a division, nor a *corps d'armée*.[1] He could not acquire that faculty of moving troops on a given ground, which is developed by daily practice, whereby the combinations are daily varied. The Italian wars offered him scarcely any application of that art, the usual actions being generally mere combats of posts, the attack or defence of defiles, and operations among the hills.

Afterwards, when he had attained the supreme power, the forces of the armies he led, requiring their organisation into *corps d'armée*,

---

1. It was General of Brigade Chanez, formerly sergeant of the French Guards, in command at Paris in the winter of 1795-6, who taught manoeuvres to General Bonaparte, at that time General-in-Chief of the Army of the Interior.

rendered a knowledge of manoeuvres less necessary. A general at the head of 80, 100, or 150,000 men only gives the impulse; he fixes on the principal points of the movements, he arranges the general conditions of the battle, he provides for the great incidents that may ensue; he is, in fact, the incarnate providence of his army. The generals who manoeuvre and who fight are those in command of 30,000 men, and the generals under their orders; they must be familiar with tactics. If I enjoy some reputation in regard to that, I owe it to my long sojourn at the camp of Zeist, where, for more than a year, I was constantly engaged in instructing excellent troops, and in learning myself with all the zeal and fervour given by a first command-in-chief to one in the prime of youth.

Tactics has the same aim as strategy, but on a smaller scale and on a different stage. In place of operating on a large expanse of country and for days together, we act on the field of battle, the whole of which is within our view, and the movements are accomplished in a few hours. The basis of the combinations, the object proposed, are always to be stronger than the enemy on a given point of the battle. Talent consists in bringing up unexpectedly to the Most important and accessible positions, the means of destroying the equilibrium and giving the victory; in fact, in executing with promptitude, movements which disconcert the enemy and take him by surprise.

In order to do this, it is essential to employ our reserves at the proper moment; in that consists the genius of war. We should carefully avoid bringing them into action too soon or too late; in the former case, we should be uselessly wasting our means and depriving ourselves of them at the moment when they would be most necessary; in the latter, we should be allowing the victory to remain incomplete or the defeat to become aggravated and irreparable.

We should compel everyone to expend all the energy he possesses; this is followed by exhaustion, and it is at this moment which it is so important to perceive, that succours should arrive, moreover, they axe certain to be demanded before they are urgently necessary.

Napoleon was very skilful in this respect, he clearly perceived the turning point of the battle. At Lutzen, he gave me a great proof of this. The battle came on unexpectedly. Believing that the enemy had retreated, the emperor had departed for Leipzic with two *corps d'armée*, and had enjoined on me to make a reconnaissance in strength on Pegau. Setting out from Wippach, where I had passed the night, I judged it prudent to make my movement by the right bank of the ravine, although this was the longest road: I was anxious to avoid endangering my communications with the main body of the army, which owed its salvation to this circumstance.

I arrived at Starsiedel in battle array, at the very instant when the enemy having surprised the 3rd corps was on the point of surrounding and then destroying it. I had just time to cover it partially and to protect its right flank, whilst it ran to arm itself. The battle came on immediately; immense masses of troops, an enormous number of cavalry, and a considerable force of artillery attacked us. Whilst the 3rd corps sustained an obstinate infantry combat at Kaya, Napoleon hastened to that point. The forces in front of me continuing to increase, I sent to him for reinforcements; he replied that the battle was at Kaya and not at Starsiedel, and he was right. I had prevented the battle being lost at its commencement, but it was at the centre it was won.

In some other circumstances Napoleon acted with less judgment. At Borodino, he showed a fatal circumspection in refusing to allow his guard to advance, when at two o'clock General Belliard asked him to do so. The Russian army was then in the greatest confusion, immense results would have been obtained by fresh troops; one hour's respite saved the enemy.

Here Napoleon acted in opposition to one of his favourite principles which I have heard him enunciate more than once, it is, "that those who retain fresh troops for the morrow of a battle are almost always beaten." He added, "we should, if useful, bring up our troops to the last man, because on the morrow of a complete success we have no more obstacles before us, opinion alone will suffice to secure new triumphs for the conqueror."

So also at Waterloo, Napoleon brought his guards too late into action. If it had advanced while the cavalry were performing prodigies of valour, the English infantry would have probably been overthrown, and the French army having got rid of the English, could have met, fought, and defeated the Prussians.

To resume—tactics may be defined as the art of movements executed in the presence of the enemy with the formation that offers the greatest advantages, and which is more in harmony with circumstances.

CHAPTER 5

On Manoeuvres

Manoeuvres are the means employed by tactics. They consist in the art of moving masses, and of making them pass, quickly and without confusion, from the order of march to the order of battle, even under fire, and *vice versâ*.

We may fight and we may march with all sorts of formations; but some formations are preferable to others both for fighting and for marching, and those for fighting vary according to circumstances.

Thus we deploy, when we have to receive the enemy in position and he is advancing, in order to expose him to an extensive fire, otherwise he would approach almost without damage. If we advance upon the enemy, we may also deploy; but this has its dangers, on account of the waving which an advance in order of battle always occasions, and of the disorder which may result from it. Hence it is preferable to have only a portion of our troops deployed, and to mix them up with columns, which are so many compact points where the authority of the officers has less difficulty in maintaining order. Such was the formation in which the right and centre of the French army of Italy traversed, in 1797, the extensive plains of the Tagliamento in presence of the Austrian Army.

The attack of a position requiring the most rapid advance, and the ground to be got over often abounding in obstacles, the troops should always be formed into columns by battalions. These small masses are easily moved, they have no difficulty in passing through all the defiles; the rear, less exposed to the enemy's fire than the van, pushes on the latter, and we thus arrive more quickly.

To make this disposition complete, a large number of skirmishers should precede the columns, and advance in a direction corresponding to the intervals between the battalions, so as to divide the enemy's fire and to cover the deploying if that is necessary, without masking the heads of the columns, which may immediately commence their fire. The skirmishers so placed find themselves supported; they have stated and accessible rallying points, and they can never be compromised.

The formation in square is but accidental, and serves in an open country to resist the attacks of a numerous cavalry. As this formation scarcely harmonizes with the movements, and does not suit an engagement against infantry, the troops should be trained to pass with the greatest rapidity from the order in line to that in column, and *vice versâ*.

In Egypt, however, we have seen troops formed in squares for marching, and keeping this formation during whole days. But there were two reasons for this: it was desirable to inspire the soldiers with confidence to resist the impetuous attacks of a new enemy, and to protect the sick, the wounded, and the artillery. A superfluous, I might almost say a ridiculous thickness was given to the squares, the men being placed in six ranks. True, what was exaggerated in these precautions was soon abolished, and squares of three and even two ranks were adopted: moreover, this formation was not had recourse to until an immediate charge of the enemy was expected.

In general the march in squares is detestable; after a short time it occasions disorder; for the conditions of marching are not the same on the different sides of the square, some march in order of battle while others perform a march of flank.

CHAPTER 1

On the Organisation and the Formation of Troops

The organisation and the formation of troops are not arbitrary matters; their object is to render a reunion of men compact and to make them into a whole, a unity which shall be moveable: the rules for doing this are deduced from certain conditions determined by the faculties of man and by the nature of the arms he employs.

In order to form troops, the first thing required is to establish order and to secure obedience. For this end a system of classification and successive bonds of union have been invented, which, when combined with skill, subject a large mass of individuals to the action of authority.

SECTION 1.—OF INFANTRY

At first there was formed a small company, easily commanded; several such companies were then united and their chiefs subjected to the control of a superior chief; in this case the unit is no longer one man, but an assemblage of men. Thus a squad, composed of eighteen or twenty men, is under the command of a sergeant, aided by corporals; a union of squads form a company, commanded by a captain, assisted by officers; several companies united form another mass, termed a battalion. The chief, coming in contact with only four, six, or eight men, commands through the medium of the latter, and thus acts upon the whole.

The company is the element of organisation, discipline, and administration; the battalion is the real military element in infantry, the unit for the battles: we move and we manoeuvre by battalions, and with battalions we fight.

As to the strength of the battalion it may vary, but only within certain limits depending upon the nature of things; we must not take literally the proverb, "The God of armies is on the side of large battalions"; this proverb, moreover, was doubtless intended to apply to large armies, a part standing for the whole. Two conditions are to be observed in the numerical composition of the battalion. It should be mobile, and when deployed, the voice of its commander should be audible at both extremities. Within these limits we add more or retain fewer companies, increasing the numbers in each in the latter case.

There should be a certain proportion between the number of officers and soldiers. Experience has shown that the proportion which best unites economy with efficiency is one officer for every forty soldiers, or twenty-five officers for a battalion of 1,000 men. The only disadvantage of a greater number of officers is the expense to the state; in every other respect it is useful, whether by multiplying the means of action or. superintendence and the examples of bravery, or by making rewards more attainable by a more rapid promotion.

The effect of organisation differs in different nations. The strongest battalions are the Austrian, the weakest the English. The full complement in Austria is over 1,200 men: this is too large a number for efficiency: with such a number it is impossible to move with regularity and ease.

I can, however, see one advantage in this arrangement; as in time of war there are always repeated losses, and as it is difficult to find enough men to supply them, a battalion of this strength will last longer; a great reduction of its strength does not incapacitate it for service. In France the battalions have usually been weaker, and their effective force, even at the commencement of a campaign, is still almost always below the full complement of organisation.

I would limit the number of a battalion to 1,000 men; and that because this number is never preserved entire on passing from a state of peace to one of war, or quitting a garrison to enter on a campaign. According to invariable experience the best and most efficient body under those circumstances undergoes a diminution of one-fifth by soldiers in hospital, workmen who remain with the *depôt*, men employed about the baggage, &c. Thus a battalion of 1,000 men has not more than 800 under arms; after a few months of campaigning it is reduced to 500, which is still a sufficient force before the enemy. The formation adopted for the battalions also influences their numerical strength.

In all the continental armies the infantry is formed in three ranks: in England only in two. This latter formation appears to me preferable. There is nothing to justify a third rank. Without entering into details respecting firing, I shall appeal to experience. On the parade ground it is possible to fire in three ranks, but not on the field of battle. The French rules say that the muskets of the first ranks are to be passed to the third rank, which is to do nothing else but load the arms. This is mere theory, quite inapplicable in presence of the enemy, and in practice it has been completely abandoned. When in position the fight is carried on by discharging the musket. The best formation, therefore, is, that which offers the most facilities for firing, which gives it the best direction and the greatest development. The fact is, that the third rank soon passes spontaneously into the other two: instinct leads the men to take the most advantageous formation but this change taking place irregularly produces a sort of disorganisation; it would therefore be much better to ratify this formation and render it permanent.

The object of arranging troops in three ranks was doubtless to give them greater consistency for the march in line, but it does not suffice. Even with three ranks, a line in movement has little solidity; and for the march in line I would prefer a deeper formation. At all events, with a slight modification, the formation in two ranks fulfils all the conditions required.. I shall explain how.

When in position, troops so arranged have a front one half larger. For the march in line, cause the first and fourth grand divisions to fall back behind the second and third, and you have thus four ranks; and when you halt you will present a front one fifth less, it is true, than by the ordinary arrangement, but in two minutes you may double it. Thus we have for the march a solid and compact formation, which allows a battalion to fire in all directions, in the event of an unexpected charge of the enemy's cavalry which surrounds it, and all this is done by facing about the first and fourth grand divisions, which are in rear of the second and third. The formation in two ranks, thus disposed, appears to me to be incontestably the best for an advance in line.

After the formation of the battalion comes that of the regiment. In this case everything is arbitrary, and depends on the fancies of the authorities. A regiment may consist of two, three, four, five or six battalions; it is simply a question of administration and economy.

Regiments composed of several battalions have an equal number of men at a smaller cost; fewer staff officers are required, and the advantages of association are reaped by greater numbers. A regiment thus composed has generally a better feeling, a more energetic *esprit de corps*, because it has more individuals co-operating for its reputation and glory; it has more *éclat* in public opinion, because its numbers place it in a position to perform by itself the greatest deeds. In wars of invasion, in the occupation of extensive countries, regiments thus constituted may form *échelons* to collect the men left behind. These *échelons* may receive recruits, drill them, and furnish supplies to the battalions in front of the enemy. Thus a great economy of men is obtained, an economy not inferior in importance to that of money.

In general, the regiment is essentially an administrative formation; it is bound together by a sort of social constitution, animated by a spirit at once patriotic and paternal.

The regiment is a kind of city, of which the colonel is the father—the magistrate. Without depreciating courage—the first of military virtues—we may say that the essential qualities of a colonel, those which have most influence in making a good regiment, are not so much any extraordinary degree of bravery as a spirit of order and of justice, and great firmness. The best regiments are those which have a commander of this sort.

Theoretically, a regiment of infantry ought to be instructed for all services, and the conditions and exigencies of war require each regiment to have a light infantry of its own. Still, special corps have been judged necessary, and this is my opinion also. For advanced guards, for detachments in broken and mountainous country, we require men of a particular kind of intelligence, endowed with a sort of instinct for overcoming obstacles—who, being trained so as to possess great skill, are able to fire with a more fatal aim. But, in my opinion, in no army have the true principles been acted on.

In France and Russia there are regiments of light infantry; these corps, except in name and dress, scarcely differ in any way from ordinary regiments of the line.

The "*Chasseurs de Vincennes*" have been lately established[1] in France. This is a good institution, but incomplete in so far as the battalions composing the corps are not divided into war and garrison battalions, in accordance with the principles I shall presently lay down.

In Austria there are battalions of *chasseurs*. In England there are companies belonging to a regiment which never leaves the *depôt*. Both these plans are better than ours, but they, too, require some modifications.

---

1. Marmont wrote this in 1846. Now, all European powers have light infantry armed with the rifle.

The infantry regiments have their light companies; in so far, therefore, an immediate want is already supplied. In our selection of men from the central companies we may always choose those who are most capable of doing good service.

The special corps of light infantry ought to have a numerical strength proportioned to the wants of large advanced guards and to the requirements of mountain warfare.

Regiments consisting of several battalions are too strong for this service; and as it requires great subdivision of the men, one chief cannot command a large number of them. Therefore, an organisation should be adopted which shall present to the enemy only one strong battalion.

This is the case for very strong companies. I should like a battalion of light infantry to consist of 1,200 men, formed by six companies of 200 men each, commanded by five officers. But it will not suffice that these troops have only a particular kind of instruction and a special formation; they should be stronger and younger men than the others. The right selection of the men is of great importance.

In forming a new corps, you may constitute it in the most satisfactory manner; but after a few years you will have heavy frames for setting your young soldiers in, and the corps will have lost all its agility.

The corps of light infantry must be composed of two battalions— one of 1,200 men, to be always maintained at full strength, and ready for active service—the other of four companies, composed of 600 or 800 men, which I may call the garrison battalion, for instructing recruits, for receiving all the men still fit for service but not suitable for a war of advanced posts, which requires so much strength and youth. I perceive another advantage in such a disposition: the general has thus at his disposal very good troops, which he may employ to do garrison work in fortified places or posts threatened by the enemy.

I am quite aware that great objection may be felt to employing on such service a good regiment or part of a good regiment, capable of taking the field; and yet it is an absurd and fatal error to confide their defence to bad troops. The latter would surrender the place to the first onslaught of the enemy, and thus the general would lose the point of support on which he reckoned at the very time it was most required.

In Spain, I twice had the mortification of being exposed to this misfortune. General Dorsenne had formed the garrison of Ciudad-Rodrigo with negligence, and this place, which had resisted the French Army for twenty-five days after the trenches were opened and the most powerful means employed, was taken in four days by the English, whilst the army of Portugal was hastening to its assistance. Subsequently I caused the passage of the Tagus at Almaraz to be fortified with the greatest care in order to keep open the communications of the army of Portugal with that of the South of Spain. Works, riveted with masonry and provided with redoubts, covered the left bank; advanced forts defended the only passage by which the enemy's artillery could pass. This post of Almaraz was of great importance; I had placed garrisons there of sufficient strength. But the troops were of mixed character, and the bad ones were in a majority, especially a German battalion called *Prussian*. The good troops occupied the advanced posts which defended the Col of Mirabete.

The enemy appeared unexpectedly: the English column which brought the artillery halted and could not pass. But another column having crossed by bye-ways the girdle of rocks that bounds the plain, came up with ladders and scaled the works. The slightest resistance would have sufficed to repel such an audacious attack executed in broad daylight. The commander of the fort. Major Aubert, a brave soldier, mounted the parapet to encourage his frightened troops; he was slain; his death spread consternation among his men, and the garrison fled to the other side of the Tagus, abandoning the fort to the enemy, who retreated after having destroyed the defences.

Section 2—Of Cavalry

In cavalry, as in infantry, we should above all things aim at order, obedience, mobility; but the mode of fighting and the character of the weapons not being alike in these two arms, the technical details are entirely different.

Fire-arms in the cavalry are almost a superfluity; they are seldom of any use beyond making signals.

Cavalry is designed to fight man to man; it should cross weapons with the enemy, dash against, overthrow and pursue him; its most frequent occupation is to pursue the enemy; it rarely happens that two bodies come in contact Before that happens, the one that has least confidence stops and takes to flight.

The movements of this arm should always be rapid and impetuous; sometimes even, but only in the case of small bodies, it may display a boldness verging on imprudence.

The French cavalry is the first of the world in battle; it always charges through thick and thin. It may occasionally fall a victim to its rashness; but, generally speaking, what favourable results have been gained by this impetuosity! In our first immortal campaigns in Italy what thousands of prisoners did not a mere handful of dragoons sometimes secure!

In order to command cavalry, where large masses are to be used, superior qualities and peculiar talents are required. Nothing is rarer than a man who knows how to manoeuvre, lead and make use of them at the proper moment. In the French army we have had three such men during twenty years of warfare: Kellerman, Montbrun and Lassalle.

The qualities required by a general of cavalry are of so varied a nature, and are so rarely met with in the same person, that they almost seem to be mutually antagonistic.

There must be, first of all, a sure and ready "*coup-d'oeil,*" a rapid and energetic decision, which must not exclude prudence; for an error, a fault committed on commencing a movement is irreparable, owing to the short time required for performing it. The case is different with the infantry, whose movements are always slow compared with those of the general and his staff.

The general of cavalry should make it his study to shelter his troops from the enemy's fire while they are in position, but not to spare them when the moment has come for the attack. On the eve of the battle, and until he has to fight, he should provide for the wants of men and horses with the greatest care; he should maintain his forces in the highest state of perfection; but when the moment arrives he should be lavish of his troops, without giving a thought to the losses he may have to sustain; his only consideration should be how the greatest possible advantage is to-be gained.

It scarcely ever happens that a general fulfils in an equal degree both these conditions. One is, perhaps, an excellent administrator and preserves his troops, but having his thoughts too much directed to that point, he dares not throw them upon the enemy, and they prove useless on the field of battle. Another is always ready to bring them into action, but is so little careful of them in a campaign that they perish from neglect before they have seen the enemy. To give two examples: a want of care may be charged to Murat, the opposite extreme to General —— who commanded the cavalry of the imperial guard after Bessières was wounded at Wagram. If he had charged at the moment when the offensive movement of Macdonald, aided by the artillery of the imperial guard, routed the right of the Austrians, 20,000 prisoners would have fallen into our hands.

Cavalry having to assail the enemy, and the men to fight hand to hand, cannot and must not ever fight in columns. This formation may serve to facilitate its march; but the instant it comes near the enemy it should deploy. A column of cavalry surrounded is soon destroyed, for there are but few soldiers capable of using their weapons. Deployed cavalry should be formed in two ranks, so as to arrest the disorder that may occur in the first rank. Formerly it used to be formed in three lines, but it was not long before the error of that formation was discovered.

The unit of cavalry in fighting order is called squadron; the rule for determining its strength is to combine the greatest mobility with the maintenance of order.

A squadron with too large a front would be easily thrown into disorder by the smallest obstacle, and every troop in disorder is already half defeated. Experience has shown that the best formation—that which combines the greatest strength and consistence with great mobility—is a squadron of forty-eight files, divided into four divisions of twelve. Divisions of sixteen and eighteen files are also suitable at the commencement of a campaign, especially among light troops, whose more active service and numerous detachments tend to weaken the corps.

The small number of men and horses allows us to do with the cavalry what cannot be done with infantry; thus the unit of battle is the same as the unit of administration.

Generally speaking, ideal perfection for service would demand an organisation of all arms applicable to the field of battle and to their daily existence—I mean to the police of the barracks, to the administration, and to the manoeuvres—on organisation which would retain the men always in the hands of the same chiefs, and thus give it greater stability and power.

Formerly, a squadron was composed of two companies. By this arrangement, one of the two captains was placed under the command of the other. This was a faulty disposition. He who is in command should have a constant and fixed superior social status over those who obey him—this is the fundamental principle of a hierarchy. Still we have made war with squadrons formed thus; but, since the peace, the subject has been well discussed, and all the best men now think alike. The squadron-company has been adopted, and the soldiers, in whatever position and circumstances they may be, always remain under the same chief.[2]

In the formation of a line of cavalry in order of battle there is a difference between the practice of the French army and that of the German and Russian armies. Our squadrons are placed at equal distances, whereas in Germany and Russia they are placed two and two together, so as to form a division without interval This formation, while it maintains the same mobility in the squadrons, gives more consistence to every point of the line, and in that respect has the advantage; but, on the other hand, in the French formation we have a longer front with an equal number of combatants, whereby the wings are extended. I am unable to decide which is the better of these two formations, the advantages and inconveniences of which appear to balance one another.

Cavalry is necessary in war, for the purpose of reconnoitring and getting information respecting the enemy. This is the business of what is called light cavalry; it is the eye and the ear of the army; without it a general is always surrounded by dangers.

Cavalry is also useful for fighting and for turning a victory to good account A battle won without cavalry does not afford a decisive result.

We had a proof of this in 1813, after having defeated the Russians and Prussians, at Lutzen and Bautzen, with our infantry alone. These victories produced a great moral effect, but no real advantage resulted from them. An enemy in flight can always rally, if not attacked quickly at the moment when it is in disorder.

The cavalry of the line has a two-fold object—1st, to engage the enemy's cavalry and pursue the defeated army; 2nd, to attack the infantry disposed for resistance.

In order to fight infantry, we require heavy cavalry, encased in steel, and sufficiently covered or protected from fire to be able to attack it without fear. It ought to be armed with lances and sabres; each man should have a simple pistol—there is no need for any other firearm, except a certain number of carbines per squadron, to enable each regiment to clear the way for itself when it is isolated.

There is a fourth kind of mounted troops, whose institution is of very ancient date,[3] and which has, in some unaccountable manner,

2. Lieut.-General Préval, who, under the restoration, was member of the Council of War, and one of its lights, is the author of the principal alterations which were then introduced into the organisation of the cavalry.
3. It was Marshal de Brissac who, in the 16th century, during the Piedmontese wars, organised the first corps of dragoons, which was of great use to him.

undergone a complete perversion: I refer to dragoons. Originally they were nothing but mounted infantry; they ought always to have retained that character. As such, dragoons might render immense service in thousands of circumstances; in detachments, for surprises; in retrograde movements; and especially in pursuits. But in accordance with the object of their, institution, they should be mounted on horses too small for a formation in line, otherwise the intrigues and pretensions of their colonels will soon convert them into cavalry, and they will become bad infantry and bad cavalry.

A corps ought to have a belief, a conviction, a faith, resulting from the cherished principles of even the prejudices with which their minds are imbued. But we must not confuse their understanding by giving utterance to contradictory opinions before them; for instance, when drilling them at cavalry exercise, we must not solemnly declare that cavalry ought always to beat infantry; and when we put them through then: infantry drill, tell them, on the contrary, that good infantry cannot be beaten by cavalry. When the soldier comes to their application, the axioms inculcated generally recur to his mind in an inverse manner. As a foot soldier, he remembers the vaunted prowess of the cavalry; when mounted, he does not forget how much reason the cavalry has to dread the infantry.

There is, I repeat, no more useful institution than that of dragoons, but then they must not be diverted from their right use. The horses should be small, as I have already stated; their harness and the equipment of both men and horses should be solely calculated for the easy and rapid service of real infantry, armed with good muskets and bayonets, and well provided with ammunition. Dragoons, in fact, should be clothed and shod so as to be able to march with facility.

As regards the cavalry properly so called, the cavalry of the line and *cuirassiers*, I would have it armed with lances, sabres slightly curved, useful for cut and thrust, and a pistol; to each squadron there should be twenty breach-loading carbines.

I have in another place discussed the question of the lance: in order not to impair the completeness of the present work, I shall reproduce here the arguments in favour of this arm, which Marshal Saxe used to call *the queen of weapons.*

I shall, in the first place, remark that it is not at all suitable for light cavalry, which having to defend itself against several enemies at once, should be provided with fire-arms and sabres. And yet it is the light cavalry that has been armed with the lance in those countries where it has been introduced.

It is well known with what facility new customs are adopted; in the most civilized countries the authority of example ensures a blind trust. No one thinks of searching for the origin, nor for the circumstances that explain a certain practice; no account is made of essential differences; hence arise erroneous and irrational applications.

Whence comes the false employment of the lance in the armament of mounted troops? From the example of warlike nations, such as the Cossacks and the Arabs. These people inhabit plains where horses are abundant; they fight without instruction and without rule, and do wonders with the lance. Looking at them as light troops, some one has said:—The lance ought to be of service in the hands of light cavalry.

No inquiry was made as to the origin of the weapon, or how it was that these nations used it so skilfully. In a barbarous country, whither the arts have not penetrated, where there are no manufactures, no stores of arms, no money to buy them with, a man gets on horseback and desires to arm himself; he cuts a long branch of a lights wood tree, sharpens its point, hardens it at the fire, and then he has a lance. He subsequently procures a nail, which he places at the end of his stick; this renders his weapon more dangerous. Finally, the branch is provided with an iron head of a proper shape, and here we have the lance, such as it has been adopted by our armies.

It is not from choice that the Cossacks arm themselves thus, but from necessity. And if they have become formidable by their skill in the use of the lance, it is because they have exercised themselves in if since their childhood.

From such examples we cannot draw any conclusion in reference to light troops, specially trained for employment in civilized countries.

The lance is the weapon of cavalry of the line, and especially of that kind intended for fighting against infantry. The sabre cannot supply its place: what use could the cavalry make of their sabres if the infantry remains firm and undaunted? The horsemen cannot cut down the foot soldier, his bayonet keeps the horse at too great a distance. On the other hand suppose the horse, the only offensive weapon of the horseman, to be killed, it falls and makes a breach in the rank, and this breach allows those near to penetrate into the squadron's ranks. The advantage is therefore all on the side of the infantry. On the other hand, suppose the same line of cavalry. to be provided with a row of pikes projecting four feet in front of the horses, the chances of success in that case will be completely reversed.

But the sabre is better adapted for light troops than the lance; in hand to hand combats a short weapon is more easily managed, and is more advantageous than a long one. Other things being equal, it is certain that a hussar or a *chasseur* will beat a lancer; they have time to parry and to strike again before the lancer who has attacked them can put himself on the defensive.

The sabre for light troops ought to be slightly curved, a perfectly straight sabre is less handy in single combat.

These troops should also be provided with fire-arms, as a supplementary means of resistance, and to enable them to be heard by the main body they are intended to guide and warn.

As regards *cuirassiers*, and all cavalry of the line, it would be better for them to have both the lance and the straight sabre. The first rank would charge with the lance in rest, the second sabre in hand. When once the shock has been given, and the ranks mixed, the sabres of the second rank will do their work.

In the days of chivalry the combatants advanced face to face, they rushed straight at one another; in that case the long weapon must have been preferable. This accounts for the use of the lance by the knights of old.

I shall relate a fact bearing out my views with regard to the mode of employing the lance, and obtaining great results from it.

In 1813, at the Battle of Dresden, at the left of the Austrian Army, our *cuirassiers* had made several chaises against the infantry which had been abandoned by the cavalry. The infantry always resisted; it repulsed our attacks, although the rain prevented almost all the muskets being fired. This resistance could not be overcome until fifty lancers, which formed the escort of General Latour-Maubourg, were placed in front of the cuirassiers; the lances made a breach, through which the *cuirassiers* were able to penetrate and destroy the enemy; True, the shots fired in this case by the infantry were very few, but under other circumstances there could be no doubt as to the result if the *cuirassiers* had been armed with the formidable lance.

The lance has also the superiority in combats of one body of cavalry against another, if opposed to an enemy armed only with sabres. It is a splendid weapon when the hostile troops come in contact. It is also useful in the pursuit of the flying enemy.

To sum up, I am authorised in saying, that for cavalry of the line, the lance should be the principal weapon, and the sabre an auxiliary arm; that for light troops the arms should consist of sabres and fire-arms. There is no doubt that routine and prejudice will continue for a long time to come to oppose these principles, the truth of which, however, appear to me to be demonstrated.

The Russian Army has a great advantage over all the European armies. The Cossacks in it form an admirable, indefatigable, intelligent light cavalry; they know how to find their way with precision, to reconnoitre the country, to observe everything, and be quite independent They cannot be compared with any light troops drilled systematically for this service; nature has formed them; their intelligence is developed by their own daily wants. I. speak now of the frontier Cossacks: constantly at war with their neighbours, always exposed to the attacks of an artful and enterprising enemy, they are obliged to be constantly on their guard.

The Cossacks of the Don, who were formerly admirable troops, have become less excellent and less intelligent since their country has only consisted of subject provinces. But there are still numerous Cossacks who guard the frontiers of Asia, on the Kouban, on the line, on the Therac, and to the east of the Caspian Sea. Russia can dispose of, for purposes of war, and could lead into Germany, more than 50,000 of this cavalry, which would allow the regular cavalry to preserve itself in good condition for the day of battle. This circumstance permits us to regard the Russian hussars and *chasseurs* as cavalry of the line, and enables them to be dispensed from the usual service of light troops; for, from want of habit and the necessary instruction, it is said that they understand nothing about the duties which are so well performed by the Cossacks.

Austria could have something analogous to Cossacks, though not on a large scale. She could easily get together 10,000 troops of this nature by forming a corps of 500 horsemen attained to each frontier regiment I cannot understand how it is that in a country where everything is co-ordinated with such care, where organisation is carried to such perfection, something of this sort has not yet been executed.

When France shall have subdued Algeria she may, without difficulty, levy Arab troops which will be of inestimable service in time of war. In order to attain this object the constant solicitude of the government is required, and it would be well to commence immediately to enrol the greatest possible number of native troops, so as to have a large number of men connected with the glory of our arms, accustomed to look upon their interests as identical with ours, to rejoice in our successes, and from among whom we may draw good non-commissioned officers, the want of whom will be felt the more this organisation is extended.

Cavalry being intended for hand to hand engagements, the question naturally occurs—why no attention is given to the protection of the men from the blows of the enemy. It would require but little to preserve them from a sabre-cut, from a lance-thrust, or even from a musket-shot fired at some distance, or a pistol-shot Eastern nations, whose combats are always *mêlées*, have always paid attention to this subject; they are often completely encased in coats of mail. The upper part of the body may be protected by means of a buffalo skin jacket, such as that used as a garment by the peasants of Castillo; for the head the *shako* may be furnished inside with two bits of wood arranged in the shape of a cross, as is often done; the limbs may be protected by one or two light iron chains placed outside the sleeves and trousers.

This durable *cuirass* of buffalo skin, braided and ornamented, would form an elegant dress, reminding us of that of the Roman soldiers; and, perhaps, it might be equally useful to furnish the infantry of the line with this light and warm dress, which while favourable to the health, protects the soldiers from the injurious effects of a sudden change of temperature. Thus the coat would be reduced to a vest, with skirts like that of the *cuirassiers*; and the buffalo skin garment, only put on when under arms, would be the sign of actual service.

I shall add another word relative to the drilling of cavalry, which has always appeared incomplete to me. Too much value cannot be attached to good riding, nor is it possible to bestow too much pains in order to render the riders perfect masters of their horses. The man and the horse should, as it were, form but one individual, realising the fable of the Centaur.

A knowledge of riding is everything. It is that which subdues and subjects the horse. The manoeuvres will always be pretty accurately performed with soldiers who are good riders. Encouragements of all sorts should be offered, in order to attain this object. We must accustom the troops to charge at full speed, without bestowing too much pains to keep exactly in order, which would be impossible with that impetuosity which is the best mode of overcoming the enemy; but at the same time, we must accustom them to rally at the first signal with promptitude and dexterity. We must continually keep this circumstance before them, and prepare them for it by all possible means. If we do so, then the apparent disorder of the charge will have no bad effect on their morale.

If, on the contrary, the charges practised at drill are moderate, they will be still less animated in presence of the enemy, and will never succeed in overthrowing him; on the first appearance of disorder the soldiers will imagine themselves lost. If drilled as I have described, they will regard this disorder as something quite usual, easily set to rights, and not at all dangerous.

There is a common practice at drill, in great manoeuvres and sham-fights—a body of infantry is charged by cavalry, and as it is merely the representative of a combat, the cavalry stops before reaching the infantry, or charges through the intervals. Nothing can be worse than this education for the horses; if we thus accustom them to avoid the obstacle, we shall never be able to make them overthrow it, for the habit in which we have trained them will be in accordance with their instincts, and perhaps with those of their riders. This practice is pernicious, it ought to be banished from our exercises and an exactly opposite lesson substituted; the results would be immense in actual war. This is what I would propose:—Draw up a line of infantry in front of a line of cavalry, place the men in both lines at such a distance from one another that a horse and a man may easily pass through the lines.

The cavalry advances first at the marching pace and passes through the infantry; it then rushes. through several times at the trot and at the gallop, until the horses execute the movement, so to say, by themselves. Then let the movement be accompanied by discharges of musketry along the line, and subsequently by broken firing, and, if a still greater noise is desired, the line of infantry may be formed in six ranks, which will produce the same noise as that occasioned by the fire of a whole battalion. After several days of such drill, cavalry will be much better prepared to attack infantry, and horses trained and used to rush upon soldiers discharging their fire-arms in front of them, will carry on their riders of their own accord, if the latter are disposed to moderate their ardour.

CHAPTER 2

Of Artillery

The third arm indispensable for war, is artillery. It is of the highest importance; but the good service obtainable from it depends particularly on its organisation, and on the principles on which it is constituted.

I shall now attempt to establish these principles, and to develop their consequences. I shall commence with the material, and thence pass to the modes of employing it with best effect

The most simple artillery is the best. If one and the same calibre could answer all purposes, and one kind of carriages suffice for all guns, that would be perfection. But this is far from being the case. Artillery has to produce effects of a great variety of kinds. When we have ascertained what these kinds of effects are, we must determine the calibres suitable for their production, limiting ourselves to the number strictly necessary; for wherever two different calibres may answer the same purpose, one of these is superfluous, and hence hurtful, on account of the complication it introduces into the munitions and the spare stores.

Artillery should be divided into three kinds—siege artillery, field artillery, and mountain artillery. In each of these divisions, and in spite of the varieties necessarily existing in the weight and dimensions of the pieces, we should as much as possible adopt the same calibres, so as to be able to use the same munitions.

In sieges and the defence of strongholds we require pieces of ordnance which will kill men, dismount the enemy's guns, and have a long range. Experience has shown that the calibre of 12 perfectly answer these purposes.

Again, in this kind of warfare we have to destroy ramparts, to knock them down, and to open a practicable breach to enable us to penetrate into the place. For this we do not want a killing weapon; what we require is an instrument, a machine, the battering-ram of the ancients, only much more powerful and expeditious in its action. To obtain this effect the calibre of 24 is absolutely indispensible. That of 16, formerly in vogue, is superfluous; too small for the one purpose, and too large for the other.

Field artillery must follow troops in all their movements, and come up rapidly to a point fixed upon, in order to crush the enemy. What we require then are light pieces of ordnance, easy of locomotion, and so mobile that they cannot be arrested by any obstacle on the ground they have to traverse. I believe the best size to be the 6-pounders, used all over Europe, and which I caused to be adopted when I was at the head of the French artillery. This is the size of gun with which all the battles of the empire were fought Eight-pounders have been subsequently adopted. Their superior size, no doubt, gives certain advantages; but they have this great inconvenience, that they increase by one-third the weight of the munitions, and thus render necessary more extensive means of transport, of which there is always a deficiency in time of war.

A second object in field warfare is to produce great effects by means of powerful reserves; to suppress the fire from field-works which support the enemy; to arm such as we have thrown up; to destroy walls; and to protect the passage across rivers. To do all this we require 12-pounders, but not such heavy pieces as are employed for the siege or for the defence of fortresses. Lastly, there may be in the rear of armies one or two batteries of short 24-pounders, intended to be fired with charges less than the third of the weight of the shot, and which, on the battlefield, will be of great service under very many circumstances.

The size of the bore of guns should, as we have just shown, be proportioned to the effects intended to be produced; and notwithstanding their large number, they may be reduced to three, with variations in the dimensions and weights of the pieces. Nor is this all. Hollow projectiles, bombs and shells are employed; their calibres should correspond as much as possible with those of the guns, which is not a difficult matter to arrange.

The shells of five inches and five lines diameter, which is the diameter of 24-pounder balls, are everywhere adopted; they possess this advantage, that they may be used indifferently in howitzers or in cannons. A larger size has been recommended for siege howitzers. They have been made 8 inches in diameter, so as to be used in the 8-inch mortar, so much employed in attacking and defending fortified places.

There are, besides, other mortars of larger calibre. The larger the calibre, the greater will be the effect produced.; The expense and the difficulty of transporting munitions for them are the only things against them. Mortars intended to receive a very large charge, cast upon a plate which supports them, and which used to go by my name, as also those termed *à la Villantroy*, are only applicable to the defence of coasts, on account of their immense weight, and because the chief object sought to be obtained from them is to throw their shot to a very great distance, which is not required in the siege or defence of fortresses.

Further on I shall have occasion to speak of a new invention in artillery, and it will be seen that the principle of the unity of calibre has been attended to in the construction of arms employed to produce different effects. The calibres I have just alluded to are, then, the only ones necessary in siege and field warfare.

There remains to be spoken of the artillery stated for mountain warfare. Without entering into details, I shall only say, that it ought to be composed of pieces of ordnance light enough to be carried on the backs of mules; larger guns, requiring carriage transport, cause more embarrassment than they render service. Congreve rockets are also extremely useful for employment in mountainous districts. I shall have occasion hereafter to speak of this invention.

There is another weapon which may be employed with much advantage, I mean wall-pieces. Their invention is not of remote date. They are loaded at the breach, and throw balls weighing several ounces, with great accuracy of aim, to a distance equal to artillery of small bore. These pieces, supplied in the proportion of ten or twelve per regiment, and generally carried together with their ammunition on a single waggon, might occasionally be of great use.

Having spoken of the size of the bore of cannons, and of the reasons for their selection, we shall now say a few words about the other dimensions of pieces of ordnance, and about their weight. The determination of these points is not arbitrary; it depends on certain circumstances, which have a direct influence on their efficiency.

The length of a cannon bears a relation to the charge it is to be loaded with. The precise limit which experiments have shown to give the greatest range has not been adopted in practise in order to avoid other inconveniences, but it has been adopted as nearly as possible. The gas formed by the combustion of the gunpowder (the explosion of which produces the force that propels the shot, acts as a spring re-coiling. As long as it acts on the moving ball, it increases the force that propels it, and, consequently, the range of the shot: this action is the effect of the gradual combustion of the powder. If the combustion has not ceased by the time the shot has issued from the gun, the range is diminished; if it takes place too soon, and the ball receives its whole impulse before having traversed the whole length of the gun, there is also a diminution of range occasioned in this ease by the friction. The quantity of powder should be such, that the expansion of gas it pro-duces in its combustion should accompany the shot from the bottom of the breach to the mouth of the gun, neither more nor less. Thus, long pieces require larger charges, shorter ones smaller charges.

In France a uniform charge has been adopted for cannons—*viz.*, a quantity of powder one-third of the weight of the shot. A series of experiments was made to determine the length that should give the greatest range with this proportion of the charge to the shot.

A gun was cast with a length thirty-five times the diameter of its bore. Having ascertained the range, a piece of the length of one diam-eter of the bore was cut off; this gave a longer range. This operation was repeated, and it was proved that the range always increased until the length was twenty-seven diameters; after this, from twenty-six di-ameters, the ranges continually diminished. Hence, we may conclude, that the maximum range is obtained with a piece of ordnance twenty-seven diameters in length, loaded with a charge weighing one-third of the weight, of the ball.

But pieces of this length would be difficult to manoeuvre with, and in order not to exceed a medium length, that twenty-two diameters has been adopted for siege and fortress guns. For field-pieces, which require to be manoeuvred with greater facility and promptitude, the length has been reduced to eighteen diameters. Foreign nations have adopted a length of fourteen diameters.

I do not here speak of howitzers; they are intended for ricochet-firing, are constructed on quite different principles, and serve for to-tally different purposes.

I shall here make an observation founded on a well ascertained fact, the application of which is of great importance, and will cause much surprise. The powder ought to burn rapidly, but still not instan-taneously, otherwise the *vis inertiae* occasions a violent shock, which destroys the gun itself. Its action should be successive. A curious cir-cumstance gave me convincing proof of this.

General Rutti, a very meritorious officer, who was at the head of the gunpowder and saltpetre department, succeeded in manufacturing powder of most extraordinary power; and he imagined he had gained a very important result Five hundred thousand pounds of this powder had been made, and it was intended to preserve it carefully for use in time of war. Fortunately its destination was changed, and this new powder was served out for the use of the Guards during their exercises in 1828. After two days' practice, all the cannons were burst and rendered useless. Having assured myself of the correctness of the fact, I investigated the cause, which was what I have stated. This reminds us of the proverb—*"leave well alone."*

As regards the weight of guns, it may be diminished to a very considerable extent without inconvenience, as far as concerns the resistance of the metal, but the carriages suffer, and are easily broken. The force of the recoil acting on too light a mass, causes a sudden and destructive shock. After a certain limit, every pound of metal taken away from the weight of the gun should be added to the carriage that supports it. A familiar example will render this fact comprehensible. We have all seen a juggler lay on his chest a very heavy stone, and receive the blow of a hammer on it with impunity, whereas he would be much hurt if the stone were smaller.

In 1802 and 1803, when engaged in establishing the new system of artillery, which was used during the whole period of the Empire, the experiments I instituted relative to the weight of the metal of guns showed that the proportion best answering the purposes of mobility and wear is that of 120 pounds of gun metal to every pound of shot— of course, with a charge of one-third of the height of the shot.

The English attach a high value to lightness in the guns of their horse artillery. They do not, or at least they did not, fifty years ago, allow more than ninety pounds for every pound of shot, but at the same time they reduced the charge to a quarter in place of a third of the shot's weight

One word more respecting the *matériel* The gun carriages are necessary elements in the employment of artillery. By use they become worn out and destroyed, rendering constant repairs and renewals necessary. Hence the immense advantage of a perfectly uniform construction. To M. de Gribauval, first inspector-general of artillery, author of the first regular system, is due the merit of having established this uniformity. Thus the remains of a carriage constructed at Auxonne or Toulouse, may serve to repair a similar carriage built at Strasburg. But the pedantry of the master mechanics, by whom he was guided, led him to adopt, in the construction of the different parts, many useless divisions and subdivisions, and hence he established in a systematic manner an embarrassing intricacy, almost as bad as the concision he had just emerged from.

In order to convey an idea of this, I shall relate one single circumstance that occurs to my remembrance. There were, if my memory does not deceive me, twenty-two kinds of wheels in his system of artillery. In the system of 1803, I reduced their number to ten. Now it has been still further reduced to four or five, and it is my belief that the *matériel* has never been so perfect as it is at presents Should a war occur now, fifty guns well commanded, will produce a greater effect than one hundred on the old system.[1]

The only exceptions I make in my eulogy of the new artillery are the adoption of the 8-pounder size, which has been condemned, and the enormous weight of the field pieces, which has been fixed at one hundred and fifty pounds to one pound of the shot.

But the best materiel in the world will produce but indifferent results, if it be not in the hands of those able to make the most of it; and though great attention has ever been paid in France to the instruction of the corps of artillery, it was still defective in many points; its organisation was very imperfect.

The imperfections I allude to have been successively remedied, and now all the conditions demanded by the best service are apparently fulfilled.

The unit for fighting purposes in artillery is the battery. It is composed of six or eight pieces of ordnance, always moving together with their munitions, and placed under the same command. The battery is to artillery what the battalion is to infantry, and the squadron to cavalry. This body must therefore be homogeneous and compact, the elements composing it must be animated with the same spirit, and must be used to act together.

There are three distinct elements: the *matériel*, or the arm properly so called, those that serve it, and those that move it. If these elements do not harmonise, the artillery is imperfect.

Next to the bravery of the gunners and the precision of aim, the most important point in regard to artillery is its mobility. Hence we perceive how important it is that the horses intended to draw the guns

---

1. Marshal Valée, formerly Central Inspector of Artillery under the Restoration, is the author of the beautiful system of artillery at present in use in France. (1846.)

be well driven.

In former days everything was divided; the guns remained in the arsenal or the park, until they were required for an engagement; the horses belonged to a contractor, and their drivers were his servants, who were treated without the slightest consideration, and who had no hope of promotion; they were termed *"charretiers"* (wagoners).

It was with such a monstrous organisation that we made all the campaigns of the Republic.

Under the Consulate and during the Empire, this service was rendered honourable, and a corps of artillery train was formed with its commissioned and non-commissioned officers. There was thus a prospect of advancement offered, and the name of "soldier of the train" was substituted for that of *charretier*. This organisation was effected by my direct influence, and was in great part my own work. In order not to interfere with the rights of different grades in as far, as the command was concerned, I took care that the officers of the train should rank very much below those of corresponding grades in the artillery corps.

By this arrangement all confusion and conflict were avoided among the officers attached to batteries and those connected with the train in their mutual relations—a most indispensable necessity. The latter not having had a competent education could never possess the superior authority; and this difference of rank kept them always, and that naturally according to the military hierarchy, in a position of obedience. This organisation lasted during the whole period of the Empire. Towards the end of the Restoration the Council of War, of which I was one of the vice-presidents, under the *Dauphin*, changed the artillery organisation. They divided it into batteries, each having its own *matériel*, guns, and horses, driven by gunners of the second class, who are also taught to manoeuvre and to serve the guns; they are called *"cannonier-conducteurs."* This organisation is certainly perfect

Within the last few years two kinds of artillery have been introduced, whose effects, if I mistake not, will be most marvellous in the first war in which they are properly used; they are the Congreve rockets for the field, and the pieces of ordnance called Paixhans guns, for defending sea coasts and fortresses, I firmly believe that they will add much to the powers of resistance of fortified places. The mode of carrying on war and the organisation of our armies will be much modified by their introduction. But these two objects deserve that we should consider them more in detail.

The part artillery has to play in war is ever becoming more and more important on account not only of its augmentation, but also of its great mobility, which permits of an infinite number of combined movements. Still there are limits to this mobility which enables us to bring a great mass of artillery to bear on a given point. The number of guns we can employ in war is also limited, owing to the expense and the difficulties entailed by an excessive amount of *matériel*; indeed these difficulties may be so great during marches, that the inconvenience they occasion may greatly outweigh the advantage they may afford in action. Experience has shown that the *maximum* ought to be four guns to every 1,000 men. This proportion, however, is soon altered by a few months of campaigning, for the materiel is not subject to the same causes of diminution as the infantry and cavalry, and the small number of artillerymen is easily kept up.

But the Congreve rockets, which have gradually been brought to great perfection, and which can now be thrown with great precision, constitute an artillery that may some day become a principal arm by reason of the development they are susceptible of.

As this arm consists merely of the projectiles used; as no machine is necessary in order to fire them, and no surface is offered against which the enemy can direct his blows; as in fine, by means of a very simple arrangement, we may instantaneously increase the fire to such a degree that the front of a single regiment may be covered by a shower of balls equivalent to the fire of a battery of one hundred guns; it is plain that the means of destruction are such, that no opposition is possible if we follow the rules and principles which the present condition of the art of war has consecrated.

The plan I would adopt with respect to the Congreve rockets is as follows. I would have five to six hundred men in each regiment instructed in the use of this new arm. Two carts would suffice to carry one hundred trestles, such as are used by the Austrians; and on the order being given, these hundred trusties, each served by three or four men, would produce a fire of which scarcely any idea can be formed.

Could, then, large bodies of troops be opposed to such a fire, even though they were formed in several parallel lines? Certainly not. But the object sought to be obtained in battle is to make the enemy fall back; we should therefore march towards him, across the space that separates us from him; and in order to do this with the least possible danger, we must employ the troops that can get over the ground most quickly. Cavalry is the best kind of troops for this purpose; and the cavalry should be manoeuvred in such a manner as to offer fewer chances of destruction from the enemy's fire. Thus it must be dispersed in skirmishing order and get ready to come together at a given signal, to be prepared for the shock of a charge. Then the infantry changes its part; it becomes the auxiliary of the Congreve rockets, or rather these rockets become its weapons, and the muskets are merely accessories.

In this novel system, the infantry requires an entire new method of instruction. It is divided into two parties: the first has charge of the rockets; the second is destined to support the first, and to serve as its rallying point when it comes into immediate contact with the enemy. The proportion of the two arms must be altered: more cavalry and fewer infantry will be required; a cavalry drilled in a peculiar way, and an *infantry-artillery*, if I may be allowed the expression, whose duties shall be limited to serving, supplying, and supporting the rockets, to occupying entrenched posts, to defending fortresses, and to carrying on mountain warfare.

But this new kind of artillery is of great importance in many instances where the ordinary artillery cannot act. In mountain districts, at present, it is with great difficulty that a few pieces of ordnance are transported, and these produce but little effect In the rocket we have a weapon with a long range which may be placed, and that in any number, upon the rocky tops of hills as well as on lower ground. In level plains every edifice may be transformed into a fortress, and the roof of a village church may become the platform of a formidable battery. In a word, this invention, such as it is, and in the state of perfection it has already attained, is adapted to all circumstances, to all combinations, and may yet influence materially the destinies of the world.

Served by a special corps, considered merely as a kind of artillery, rockets will be necessarily but rarely used, and will have very little effect. It is only by giving them an immense development that they can be usefully employed, then alone can they be made to astonish, to terrify and to crush; they should, therefore, become the arm of the whole army.

It is only by degrees that we are able rightly to consider the nature of things. We act long by routine, without troubling ourselves about possible modifications and improvements; hence it will be long ere we are able to appreciate the power of rockets. But if when war breaks out again an able and calculating general should rightly see the question in all its bearings and consequences, if he should take his measures in secrecy in order to bring them into practice on the field of battle, he would obtain a success that would defy all resistance, until the enemy makes use of the same means. In making this great experiment, the personal genius of the commander will exercise a great influence on the fate of the war.

Still, rational and probable as the result I predict may be, experience alone can show in an incontestable manner the full value of this new invention. The wise man will not be absolutely convinced until the facts shall have realised his hopes, seeing that there are so many unforeseen circumstances which modify the most well-founded calculations, the most seductive probabilities.

However, the plan appears so feasible, that an able and enlightened general should, as soon as war breaks out, prepare to make use of this new arm, and astonish the enemy by its effects. Should he alone employ it, he will probably be master of the campaign, and if his adversary has been as vigilant as himself, he will at all events guard against a defeat But his foresight should embrace all the consequences of this new arm relatively to other arms, to the proportion it should bear to these, to the drill required for it, and to the mode of using it

If the success of the employment of rockets shall be proved in an actual campaign, it is evident that all armies will adopt them: in that case the equilibrium will be restored, and no one in particular will enjoy an exclusive advantage. But the art of war will be greatly modified by it. Actions fought with greater eagerness and more moral effect will render battles shorter, will diminish the effusion of blood; for that which gives us victory is not the number of men we slay, but the number we frighten.

I repeat it, the Congreve rockets ought to make a revolution in the art of war; and the genius who first shall understand their importance, and develop all the advantages attainable from them, will make his fortune and crown himself with glory. I now come to the Paixhans artillery.

Heavy artillery, in order to do what is required of it, should have a long range, and the projectiles it throws a great momentum. In order to get this great momentum there must be one of two things—either the velocity must be very great with a moderate mass of projectile, or the mass must be great with an inferior velocity, because the momentum of a body is equal to its mass multiplied by the velocity.

Hitherto a moderate mass combined with great velocity has been preferred, owing to the difficulty attending the transport of projectiles.

But if this reason holds good in the case of sieges, when the transport should be effected in a very short and limited space of time, it does not for other circumstances when there is no limit as to time or when the transport is easily effected, whatever the weight may be. In a word, for the defence of works, for arming coasts and for naval service, this artillery possesses immense advantages, which I shall proceed to analyze in a succinct manner.

1st. The resistance of the air to the movement of bodies being as the squares of their velocities, it is much less with these projectiles; hence the range and the accuracy of firing are much greater. Supposing a velocity of 1,200 feet per second for the ordinary ball, and that of 400 for the Paixhans projectile, the resistance of the air will be as 9 is to 1.

2nd. The momentum of a 24-pound shot with a velocity of 1,200 feet will be represented by the number 28,808, whilst that of the Paixhans ball of 12 inches calibre, or of 140 pounds weight, with 400 feet of velocity, would be expressed by 66,000, in other words it would be double that of the other. That of a 36-pound ball with the same velocity of 1,200 feet will be 43,000, and thus much weaker.

3rd. The destructive action being as the squares of the diameters, the ratio is here as 1 is to 4.

4th and lastly. A 36-pound ball penetrates the parapet of an earthwork or the walls of a vessel, or it sticks in their thickness. No matter where it lodges, it does no harm; and if it goes right through the side of a ship, the hole it makes is easily plugged, but a Paixhans projectile produces a very different sort of damage. In the first place, owing to its great diameter and the slowness of its motion, the effect having an inverse ratio to the velocity, momentum being the same, it destroys a larger surface; then when it bursts it makes an immense breach; if the object struck be an earthwork it will require to be rebuilt; if it be a ship, it goes to the bottom without there being any possibility of saving it.

The defence of a fortress carried on by such means raises the defence almost to an equality with the attack, and the employment of this arm at sea against ships does away with fleets and especially with the larger vessels. Indeed there are two causes for the superiority of a ship of the line over a vessel of inferior size; the ship carries guns which the planks of a frigate cannot resist, and the frigate carries guns the calibre of which is insufficient to do damage to a ship of the line. Hence a frigate is unable to fight a ship of the line because the fire of the frigate is only dangerous to the crew and the rigging, whereas the fire of the ship destroys likewise the vessel itself, and can in one moment send it to the bottom of the sea.

But when we shall be able to mount on a small steam or sailing vessel of inconsiderable force, one or two pieces of artillery, one of whose projectiles suffices to destroy the largest ships; ten such small vessels, each armed with two large guns, would soon be able to dispose of any ship they may surround. Ships which cost more than a million and a half of *francs*, in such a case, give no guarantee of durability or good service. The Paixhans artillery is therefore a death blow to the royal navy as it is at present constituted.

During the Restoration, Lieutenant-Colonel Paixhans, a very distinguished officer, first started the idea of this kind of ordnance. Louis XVIII. named a commission of generals and admirals to examine into its value, and appointed me chairman. The explanation of this system convinced me of its possibility and novelty, and I became its avowed partisan.

However, experiments were required to ascertain the range and the accuracy of this arm, and the means of performing easily the drill required in its use. The experiments made at Brest succeeded perfectly, and surpassed the author's expectations. From that period it was requisite to make changes in ordnance, which introduce immense modifications in naval warfare, rendering large ships superfluous; in the defence of coasts, which is made more easy and certain; and in the defence of fortresses, which will apparently be much prolonged. But the adoption of this new weapon must not exclude the employment of hollow shot for thirty-six and twenty-four pounder guns, since the effect of the latter, though not so great as those of the Paixhans ordnance, are always formidable to the enemy, and advantageous for defensive operations.

CHAPTER 3

On Fortifications

It would not be consistent with the plan of this work, and probably it would be beyond my powers, to enter into details on the subject of fortifications. Under this head, therefore, I shall only consider the necessities of war and the object had in view in erecting fortifications, but I shall not trench upon the engineer's department.

In former times fortified towns were formed spontaneously, so to speak. In periods of anarchy, disorder, and internecine wars, of which the middle ages give us many examples, the numerous and wealthy populations, collected together, wished to place themselves in safety. They fortified themselves by building a rampart round their town. They provided themselves with arms. The means of attack were still in their infancy, so that they found themselves thus safe from all attack.

But the discovery of artillery and the improvements effected in this art soon changed this state of affairs. The ancient fortified towns, useless against the regular means of attack, were superseded by fortifications constructed with care and at the expense of the state. And as all towns could not be fortified, the governments selected certain of them which by their importance and especially by their position demanded the greatest consideration and sacrifices. The question was then considered no longer in reference to the special interest of the towns, but chiefly in reference to the defence of the country against an external foe. However, accident was frequently the only motive that influenced the preference for particular towns to be fortified.

All great questions should be solved by principles. The end must first be recognised and indicated; then the means for attaining it will present themselves to the mind; to act otherwise is to be guided by blind chance.

Here again the resolutions formed are modified by private interests and personal influences; and we may also say by the system of war adopted in the time of Louis XIV., which was in many respects founded on error.

Certainly no one can have a greater respect for Vauban than myself, but he was more of an engineer than a general; and in making great numbers of fortresses he followed the bent of his own predilections.

This accounts for his prodigality in making fortresses. Still I am astonished at one of the acts of a man of his genius, namely, his idea of creating a very valuable material barrier on an open frontier like that of Flanders by means of a system of fortresses disposed checkerwise.

The adoption of such a system would be perfectly right for a small country like Holland, the defence of which is mostly based on natural circumstances which have been taken advantage of by art; short distances and fortresses, which give their holders the power of causing very extensive inundations, offering great obstacles to an enemy, add to the means of an army, and facilitate its manoeuvres.

But to carry out this system on an open frontier was an error that should not have been committed by a genius like Vauban. If he had not been forced to accommodate himself to exigencies of a superior order, he would, as an engineer, have yielded to the charms of, and his mania for, constructions.

The changes that have taken place in the mode of carrying on war, and particularly the strength of the armies brought into the field, have shown the vicious character of such a system of defence; and now-a-days no military man would dream of undertaking similar works.

Recognised principles allow of two kinds of fortified places: *depôt* fortresses, and strategical fortresses.

The first should be large, very strong, and not numerous. One is enough for a frontier.

They should contain material of wax sufficient for the wants of a large army that may assemble there, as artillery, reserve of firearms, and military stores of all kinds. They should have numerous workshops, an arsenal of construction, and at all times the materials for a large hospital, and supplies of food. Finally, regiments sent to such a fortress should leave it organised and armed, and all ready for service in the field.

Afterwards there should be organised in such fortresses the reinforcements and spare stores required by the army: and if the commencement of the war has been unfortunate, or if the army inferior to that of the enemy shall be obliged from the beginning to act on the defensive, it doubles its strength by resting on such a fortress, which should by preference be situated on a navigable river, in order to make it easy to procure supplies. A *depôt* fortress is also of advantage to an army operating in its vicinity, and at the same time it gives great consistency to its base of operations.

In France we have three fortified towns of this description, wonderfully well situated: Strasburg, Metz, and Lille, for the frontiers of Germany, the Ardennes, and Flanders.

At the period of our greatness we had in Italy three fortresses in *echelon* which gave us the command of the country, Alexandria, Mantua, and Venice. Had our prosperity lasted, it is very likely another fortress of great importance would have been constructed on the Save. In countries newly conquered, such fortresses are not merely fortified *depôts* for the defence of the frontier; besides that, they give the command of the surrounding territory.

After *depôt* fortresses come strategical fortresses. These serve to facilitate the movements of armies and to harass or impede those of the enemy.

They should be situated either on rivers, both banks of which they occupy, or in mountainous districts, the valleys of which they close.

A mountain chain presents great obstacles to the movements of an army. The roads crossing them can alone give passage to considerable quantities of war material; it is therefore useful to close the issues by a fortress so as to prevent the attacking enemy from making use of them, while at the same time we retain the power of employing them for ourselves.

A river forms the line of defence of an army; the enemy intends to cross it; he will have to create the means of effecting the passage, for the permanent bridges do not belong to him. The army that is acting on the defensive, on the other hand, can manoeuvre with safety on both banks, and direct all its forces against a part of those of the enemy when they are divided. If it succeed in beating the troops which remain behind and have not yet crossed the river, those which have are thereby exposed to the dangers always attending an isolated situation without communications. Generally speaking the most efficacious method in an energetic defensive warfare, consists in offensive movements of a limited character, well calculated, and executed rapidly and to the purpose.

This will suffice in the way of the general ideas that should regulate the defence of a frontier. As regards details of construction, I shall only say that, considering the progress of artillery and the facility of transporting it, it cannot be too much impressed on the minds of engineers to prepare a sufficient number of perfectly safe shelters for supplies of all characters and for a large portion of the garrison; otherwise defence is impossible.

Fortresses should besides occupy large spaces of ground by means of detached works on a systematic plan, and of sufficient strength to enable each to defend itself unaided. The general defence will thereby be facilitated, the attack rendered more difficult, and the resistance more prolonged. There was a fine example of this kind of fortification at Alexandria, in Piedmont, and, had political events permitted its employment, this fortress would have rendered great services. But since then, its great extent requiring a corresponding garrison, and the Piedmontese army being but of moderate size, it did not suit the King of Sardinia to maintain it, accordingly it has been destroyed, and nothing now remains but the citadel.

I have already explained the object of fortresses, and the conditions that should determine their construction as well as the selection of their site. I shall now speak of fortifications, the object of which is to protect an inferior army against a superior force, and to enable it to resist, in spite of the disproportion of forces. I allude to entrenched camps, intended to establish a kind of equilibrium between armies of unequal strength.

Entrenched camps are of two kinds. The first consists of a continuous line, which creates material obstacles along the whole front of the position occupied by an army; the second consists of a certain number of points fortified with care, and, if possible, made strong enough to be safe from a surprise. Capable of resisting a sudden attack, they serve as support to the troops, protect their flanks, cover a portion of their front, and render them impregnable without interfering with the freedom of their movements.

The first kind have never been attended with good results. When seriously attacked, they have always been forced. This may be attributed to two causes.

In the first place, the troops obliged to guard the whole extent are too divided. A single point carried, often suffices to cause all the others to be evacuated. In the second place, the entrenched army always considers itself inferior, and this deprives it of half its value. If one point be forced, it no longer thinks of fighting; and yet that is the very moment when it should be most certain to conquer, for it necessarily has forces superior to the enemy, who has only been able to penetrate with the head of a column, and whose supporting troops can only arrive slowly and by passing through a narrow entrance. So that it is just when it might obtain a cheap victory that the army thinks of retreating.

Examples of this are numerous. I could easily give a great many, but I shall content myself with mentioning those which are celebrated, and one of which happened under my own eyes.

The first is the capture of the lines of Turin, defended by an army of 80,000 men, attacked by Prince Eugene of Savoy with 40,000 Austrians.

The second happened at Denain, when Marshal de Villars, with a dispirited and inferior army, beat Prince Eugene.

The third is the capture of the lines of Mainz, defended by a French Army of 30,000 men, and composed of works of rare perfection—the most considerable of the kind that have been executed in modern times. Constructed under the direction of General Chasseloup-Laubat, one of the ablest of French engineers, these works seemed to be impregnable. Nevertheless, on the 8th October, 1795, two detachments sufficed to create a disorder that nothing could remedy. One of these detachments consisted of 400 men, who passed the Rhine higher up the river and behind the works, whilst the other appeared in a narrow space left between the river and the lines at the moment when a large number of troops were seen to be preparing for an attack in front.

The only sensible use to be made of such lines, is to employ them against large but bad armies, such as those of Oriental tribes. Their usefulness in such cases has always been demonstrated and acknowledged; Prince Eugene's success at Belgrade is an additional proof. Placed between lines of circumvallation raised against the garrison of the fortress and lines of contravallation facing the army of the grand *vizier*, he was able to continue the siege, hold the army in check, take the fortress, and come out of the strife victorious; but other principles must be followed against European armies.

If we allow a soldier to rely entirely for safety on a material obstacle in front of him, and if this obstacle is overcome, he no longer thinks of defending himself, and this disastrous impression is often communicated to those of higher rank. A soldier should be convinced—and he cannot too often be reminded of this—that the guarantee of victory is, before all things, in his courage, and that he ought to despise his enemy. But if, in place of obstacles which paralyse his movements, he has only supports that cover his flanks, and so protect him, he will believe himself to be invincible, and this opinion will soon be shared by his enemy; and if he resist an attack, his movements being free, he will be able to profit by a victory, and follow it up.

An army in the presence of another but stronger army, will do well to entrench itself under certain circumstances. Resting on a fortress, a river, or a mountain range, and surrounded by a greater or smaller number of defensive points, rendered as strong as possible, it will be able to make up thereby for its inferiority in number, and establish a sort of equilibrium.

This subject leads me naturally to the question of permanent entrenched camps, composed of works riveted with masonry, embracing large spaces, situated in strategical points, and traversed by a large river. In my opinion, nothing can be more valuable, nor render greater service. Several establishments of this nature, though made on very different scales and under different conditions, have been constructed in recent times. I shall speak of the two principal ones, which have attracted most attention—that of Linz, in Upper Austria, and the fortifications of Paris.

The entrenched camp of Linz is composed of forty-two towers, built with care; they occupy a circular space of more than six leagues; each of these towers is casemated, covered on the side facing the country by the command of the glacis, and its fire is entirely *rasant*. The model-tower had a deep ditch, with a counterscarp riveted with masonry and provided with a gallery of reverse; and in my opinion it was very wrong to suppress these means of safety in this system. Each tower mounts twelve pieces of heavy ordnance. The towers are all placed within view of one another, and sufficiently near to support each other. In one part of the perimeter they occupy a series of heights, faced at a distance by rugged and difficult mountains, and they end at and rest upon the right bank of the Danube, a great way above the town. On the left bank a larger height, close to the Danube (the Pessin-Berg), is occupied by an appropriate and pretty strong work, whence stretches another line of towers, embracing a large space, and also terminating at, and resting on the Danube below the town.

I shall not enter on the question of the strength of isolated towers. I believe them to be not very capable of resisting if left to themselves. But covering an army shut up in the space embraced by, them, they appear to me to be unattackable. The enemy can never dare to besiege them while they are supported by the army, and the army placed under their protection has nothing to fear.

The fundamental principle of entrenched camps of this kind is that it should be impossible to blockade them, and that they should be situated at the point of junction of numerous communications. In this respect the camp of Linz is conveniently situated, its strategical position is well chosen. Two roads, one on each side of the Danube, follow the course of this river downwards at a greater or less distance from its banks. Several roads lead to Bohemia, others go to Salsburg, the Tyrol, Styria, and Carinthia. A camp as large as that of Linz, with the obstacles presented by the country, cannot be surrounded by the enemy, and the army that it encloses can, never lose all its communications, unless the forces opposed to it are at least treble its own numbers. Hence it can always receive reinforcements and reorganise itself, until the favourable moment arrives for taking the offensive; thus the enemy would be obliged to remain in observation, for he would never dare to venture into the narrow valley of the Danube and march on Vienna with the Austrian army in that offensive and menacing position.

In fact, to do so would be madness; and if the camp of Linz had existed in 1809, Napoleon would not have gone to Vienna, or he would have done so much later. Now, in war, and for great monarchies especially, time is everything, because all that is required is to give the natural resources of the country the means of developing themselves. Therefore the entrenched camp of Linz is a good and great military conception.

In every country there are localities which might be used for similar establishments, and which would occasionally be of great utility.

The entrenched camp of Verona is made on the same principles; and, though in very different conditions, it can and ought to play an important part in the hands of a General skilful enough to avail himself of it, and at the same time a good tactician.

I come now to the defensive works executed at Paris, which have been and still are the subject of such important and serious discussions. The construction of these forts, the system of which appears to me perfect, is a surer guarantee of the independence of France against the attacks of all Europe, than would be the acquisition of several provinces, which would have only increased the distance of the frontier.

No one will deny the immense influence exercised by Paris on the destinies of the kingdom. A head, of size disproportioned to the body, but still the active focus where the intelligent minds are assembled, where an irresistible moral force is developed, where enormous treasures are accumulated, and where all that is most distinguished in the country is congregated, Paris has done an immense deal for the power, the glory and the fame of France. But her capital makes her pay dearly for these advantages, by the weight with which it crushes her when it falls. Now, interests which affect the entire kingdom and compromise its very existence, cannot be abandoned to the fate of two or three battles; either the frontiers must be extended, or the dangers to which it is exposed by the approach of an enemy must be diminished; and there was no other mode of doing this save by preparing an impregnable asylum to the French armies, unfortunate and beaten, who should meet under its walls.

Whatever may be the consequences of the most disastrous campaign, the scattered remnants of the army will always amount to 80,000 or 100,000 men, and, supported by regularly constructed forts, these 80,000 men would, be unassailable. Now, with the reserves Paris contains, such as artisans of all sorts, populations, riches of all kinds, material of all description, and with the aid of neighbouring departments, the different services of the army would soon be filled up, and the losses repaired; and in less than a month an army of 300,000 men, well equipped and with renovated courage, would be able to march against the enemy. What force would not the enemy require to resist? If he divide, he will be weak everywhere and easily destroyed; if he remain together in order to resist and fight, how will he live? And what would be his fate after the slightest check?

If, then, the enemy has advanced as far as Paris, the best thing he can do is to take himself off, before the reorganised French army can go out to meet him; and he should hasten to carry the war into the provinces and within reach of his resources. Thus the war will be carried back to the frontiers, and all returning into its natural course, there is no longer any cause for apprehending a catastrophe.

I therefore regard as of the utmost utility to the safety and defence of France, the construction of detached forts, the development of which is such that the enemy cannot present himself in force on many points at a time. But Paris should not be fortified by a continuous rampart; for it is my opinion and also that of all experienced men who are well versed in the matter, that that city is not so situated as to enable it to sustain a siege; it was sufficient to adopt such a system of defence as should for ever prevent its being besieged; and with this object in view, the only one worthy of attention, forts were enough; a continuous wall would be superfluous, and would never be of use, whatever might happen.

Chapter 4

On Administration

An assemblage of men has wants; the talent of satisfying these wants with order, economy, and intelligence, constitutes the science of administration.

The basis of a good administration is the care employed in ascertaining that the *consumption is legitimate.* Where the inspections are exact, where the number of effectives and of those present under arms is verified with precision and frequency, there are the elements of order; for the great abuses have much less reference to the price of the articles consumed than to consumptions that were never made, and yet are alleged to have been made.

In the time of the Directory, the French military administration was in great confusion, and the First Consul, on attaining to power, hastened to create a new corps, whose business it was to make inspections so as to establish order.

He made a point of treating it with great consideration, which, in turn, elicited much zeal. In the course of six months, more than 150,000 men, who had no existence, but for the greater part of whom rations, pay, and clothes were drawn, were erased from the lists.

The systems of administration vary in different countries; all are capable of yielding good results, when the numbers of effectives and of those present under arms are exactly ascertained. I shall only remark that there are (in my opinion, at least) great advantages in giving to corps the power of providing for themselves as much as possible; for as the excellence of troops is always dependent on a good administration, a great responsibility should be imposed on commanders of corps, but at the same time they should be entrusted with great powers; their operations should be overlooked, but the direction of these operations should be conceded to them. The mere responsibility to the opinion of their soldiers will be a guarantee for their zeal. Colonels detected in prevarication should be punished in an exemplary manner, but they should be allowed to enjoy the credit of any successes they may have obtained.

In France, corps are not allowed to form reserve funds, and this is a great mistake. Association has its advantages; and an able and intelligent commander of a corps, without depriving his soldiers of the enjoyment of any of their rights, could and ought to encourage economies. If they are prohibited, they will be practised notwithstanding; and as they cannot be done openly, they will often be done in a mysterious and criminal manner. If, on the contrary, they be not only allowed, but ordered, and left to the discretion of the commander of the corps, to be employed for the advantage of the regiment in accidental cases and in cases not within the provisions of the regulations, great encouragement will thereby be given, and the colonels will take the credit of an arrangement, the honour of which will accrue to them.

Two very important branches of administration, *viz.*, the hospitals and commissariat, are faulty in almost all the European armies. An enlightened government should endeavour to establish them on new principles; the art of war would thereby secure great and direct advantages, and the welfare and conservation of the men would also gain by it. I shall begin with the commissariat.

Section 1.—On Commissariat.

In treating of the victualling of troops, I shall only speak of supplying bread; it alone presents any difficulties, since supplies of living cattle can always be within reach of the consumers.

The difficulty of distributing bread with regularity to the troops is one of the greatest embarrassments of war. It is incomprehensible that so many distinguished commanders, who from this reason have been foiled or impeded in the execution of their projects, have not succeeded in solving so important, a problem. The Romans solved it; but, in general, their wars did not require such rapid movements as modern warfare.

I believe that there is a way in which the difficulty can be overcome in a perfectly satisfactory manner, and the change I am about to suggest would have a powerful influence on the art of war.

In order to receive with regularity the distribution of bread by means of the commissariat, the army must be either stationary or retreating, either remaining at the same distance from its magazines or approaching them. If, when marching forwards, it constantly increases the distance from its magazines, the operation is impracticable for any administrator, however clever he may be, for the convoys cannot go faster than the army, and they follow it at always the same distance as at the time of setting out; at each fresh dispatch of a convoy, the distance being greater, the difficulty becomes greater.

In a war of invasion the troops can only live on the resources of the country they are traversing; but the time required for making the bread in inhabited places, the ordinary inadequacy of the milk and the ovens, or their great distance from the spot, render the local resources very incomplete, and the scanty supply resulting therefrom is the cause of great suffering and disorder. Now, on the maintenance of order in every sense and manner depends the safety of armies.

The only efficacious method of ensuring to the soldier regularity in his means of subsistence, is to trust him to provide it for himself, according to some fixed rules. I have made the experiment, and the result was completely satisfactory.

War is not made in a desert; or, if it should be so for a short time, special arrangements are necessary. War is usually carried on in inhabited countries; and where people are, there must be grain to feed them. The problem to be solved is, therefore, to use the grain of which the granaries are full.

The great difficulty is to reduce the grain to flour, as I shall explain presently. Mills are required to grind the corn: life would be supported with flour alone, without converting it into bread; death by starvation is possible amid heaps of corn.

When hand-labour is scarce and dear, there is an advantage in employing powerful machines in manufactures, and in centralising the work; but when hand-labour is abundant, and costs nothing, it is best to follow an opposite course. By transferring the work from the centre to the circumference it is facilitated, and by intrusting it to those who are to benefit by it, we can be sure that it will be executed with zeal and punctuality. That granted, it is evident that soldiers' arms may be employed without inconvenience, and that it will be to their advantage to receive as a recompense for their labour the price that that labour would cost at the time.

How does it happen that in a campaign soldiers are never without soup, when they have meat, bread, and pots? The reason is that they make it themselves. If a commissary were to attempt to have it made for a whole division, or even a colonel for a regiment, the soldiers would never have any soup when on the move.

I wish to apply to bread the method that is used with regard to soup, and the soldier will never be without it I propose giving portable mills to the army. I adopted this plan in a campaign in Spain, and it succeeded perfectly. The army of Portugal, in 1812, lived in this way for six months; the only inconvenience felt was that the grinding surfaces soon got spoiled. This was remedied by supplying others of better temper; some of these were very durable.

Napoleon, hearing of those results, was struck, in the midst of the miseries of the Russian campaign—with the advantages of the plan—and he ordered a large number of these mills to be made for the grand army. Five hundred were sent to him; they arrived at Smolensk at the same time as the army, on its return from Moscow. But then there were no longer arms to move them, nor soldiers to profit by them.

The following are the requisite qualities of these mills:—

1st. They should be sufficiently light to be carried by a soldier, who should be taken off duty for that purpose—considering its importance—if the regular means of transport should fail.

2nd. They should be capable of being turned by a single man.

3rd. They should produce good flour, and four hours' work at one should suffice for the wants of a company.

The mills of the army of Portugal turned out thirty pounds of good flour per hour. It has been objected to this system that the rules of the service require the bran to be separated from the flour, and that this operation complicates the process. To this I reply, that experiments made with care have proved the uselessness of removing the bran with wheat of good quality.

Even with wheat of mediocre quality, but pure and unadulterated, the bread is always good. When the commissariat supplies bad bread, the soldier must take it and eat it, because he would starve while waiting for a fresh supply; but when the wheat given out to him is fall of dust or other foreign substance, it can be cleansed before it is used, and then the soldier will always have good bread to eat. So that, in this respect, his condition will be improved, and it will be still more so by the wages he receives for his labour, whether they be given in money or in increased rations.

But great would be the gain of the commissariat: in ordinary times it would be greatly simplified, and in time of war its service would be rendered easy. At present it costs a commander more trouble of mind to secure the means of subsistence for his troops than to do anything else, and his combinations are constantly thwarted and rendered nugatory, owing to failures in the regular distribution of bread.

We have thus a solution not only of the problem of supplying troops with their indispensable food, but of that of furnishing them with bread properly so called. A mode has been invented of constructing ovens in any kind of soil, by means of a simple excavation, entailing four hours' labour only, where two hours afterwards bread may be baked. Thus at each bivouac, flour is made in sufficient quantity for a day's consumption; and at every resting place ovens are made in the floor of a peasant's hut and bread is baked before it is required. With this arrangement the feeding of the army takes place as it were spontaneously; the commissariat is no more occupied with these details than every man is with maintaining the circulation of his blood: it is the consequence of a principle in constant action.

In times of peace, the government will have stores of wheat which it will give out to the troops. The same would take place during a defensive war. In a war of invasion, each regiment would receive daily from the administrative powers of the country it is traversing, or would take from the granaries of the inhabitants the wheat it requires. But this should be a habit contracted and carried out in times of peace; for, as a principle, the habits of peace should resemble as much as possible those of war; and this is especially true when it is a question of the introduction of a great change.

SECTION 2.—ON HOSPITALS.

Nothing is more sad than the spectacle often presented in the army by military hospitals. On a class of men who have so many claims to attention, the care bestowed is often very incomplete. Their life is one of devotion; sufferings, fatigues and dangers are what they have to look forward to. The noblest feelings animate their breasts, and these generous fellows love their chiefs, if they are only just in the exercise of their authority. Such is the spirit inherent in the warrior; and such a spirit belongs especially to the French soldier, who is a stranger to none of the honourable feelings of mankind.

There are, no doubt, vices and evil passions in armies, as there are in all assemblages of men; but there are also to be found instances of the most exalted virtues. Therefore the preservation of sick and wounded soldiers is a duty commanded by conscience and humanity. It is at the same time of great importance for the government as well as for the commander, for a preponderating number of soldiers is an element of success, and to replace them by recruits, an expensive process in itself, is far from compensating for those lost. Besides, the knowledge that if wounded he will receive the best care, inspires the good soldier with confidence and energy on the field of battle.

It might be advisable to attempt to change the spirit of the hospital administration, to devise some mode of recompense more noble than pecuniary emolument, to develop more elevated and worthier sentiments, in order the better to sustain courage and devotion.

If the functions of those to whom is confided the care of the sick and wounded were exalted, ennobled, and rewarded by public opinion, and by the pleasure that the exercise of charity and the sentiment of piety bestow, there would assuredly thence result a great gain to the sufferers. The mode of accomplishing this would be to confide to a religious fraternity, conversant with the minor functions of surgery and medicine, the care of military hospitals; not their administration, properly so called, nor the management of the funds, but a monopoly of the charge of the patients and the direction of the hospital.

A body of hospitaller friars, bound for life or for a limited time, under the direction of honoured chiefs, should be entrusted with the care of the wards and the nursing of the patients. There should be paid assistants under their orders for the coarsest and most laborious work, but still in urgent cases no work should be considered beneath the chiefs themselves. The spirit of charity would support them in their labours. A detachment of these respectable friars, to whom a number of sick was confided, would never abandon them. Their presence would inspire the patients with hope and consolation, and their holy services exercised for the benefit of all, enemies as well as friends, would be their safeguard with all European armies, should the fortune of war deliver them into their hands.

The world's esteem and the approbation of their own consciences ought to be particularly their reward. A wisely regulated hierarchy would establish blind obedience in this body, devoted to the practice of the most touching virtues. The commander of the army would occasionally invite the superior of the hospitaller friars to his table, and assign him the place of honour; he would thus confer honour on all the inferior members of the fraternity, and would pay them with this precious money, whose value may be increased tenfold accordingly as it is judiciously employed.

Thus the service of the hospitals would be performed by three bodies:—

1st. The medical men, physicians and surgeons.

2nd. The hospital corps that furnishes the material, disposes of the funds, and supplies the provisions and medical stores.

3rd. The hospitaller friars charged with the duty of nursing and tending the patients.

This last body, constituting a kind of living and energetic controlling staff for the correction of all the mistakes the administration, properly so called, might make would be at all times a guarantee for regularity and order.

The knights of Malta originated in the cares bestowed on the pilgrims who resorted to Jerusalem, and charity was their first watchword. The anarchy and disorder of the places where they were established forced them to arm themselves for their own defence; and while continuing to be hospitallers they became soldiers.

Courage and the profession of arms have always had and will never cease to enjoy an *éclat* which naturally delights the multitude, and their military character having gained the ascendency, the hospitallers changed their nature. They were originally called into existence by the wants of a certain state of society; and the fraternity I would wish to see established would do much to improve the condition of that numerous body of men who in Europe form an energetic and truly patriotic part of every nation.

It would be easy to lay down the conditions of the administration and of the service of the hospitals; but to do so would be foreign to the plan I have proposed to myself to follow.

I have long been revolving this idea in my mind, struck by the disorders I witnessed during the Empire. Under the Restoration it was not practicable in consequence of the suspicions it would have given rise to; but now, perhaps, it might be usefully and successfully carried into execution. What advantage the army of Africa might derive from its adoption!

I am quite alive to the objections that might be made to establishments of this sort, and to the difficulty of preserving harmony among three rival bodies working together for the same object; but there are already two which are far from being harmonious, and a third without adding much to the complications would be of great use in enlightening the authorities.

I am also well aware that this institution may be made

the subject of ridicule; but that I could readily brave, sustained by the conviction that it would contribute to improve the soldier's lot; a most important object, as I think, in the interests not only of the military service, but of humanity at large.

Of late years, however, the service of the hospitals has been improved by giving a military organisation to those employed in them. Degrees of rank, as among the troops, ensure future promotion to those who do their work well, and introduces a system of order, surveillance and discipline; a kind of feeling of honour should thence spring up and authority will be more easily exercised. Good effects should follow from this.

Generally speaking, military organisation secures a regular action of the authorities at all times; it constitutes essentially a potent means for maintaining order; it may always be successfully employed, if we desire to act upon assemblages of men intended to work towards the same end; and the more confusion there exists among the primary elements, the more profit and advantage shall we derive from military organisation.

One word more about hospitals.

Miserable and mendacious calculations of economy respecting the daily cost of a man in hospital have often led to too great restrictions in the number of these establishments; and the desire to impose upon others those cares which are our duty, lead to their too frequent clearing out. Nothing can be more disastrous than these two systems when they are not necessitated by imperious considerations, such as the vicinity of the enemy or the absolute want of means. In ordinary circumstances it is impossible to make hospitals too accessible to the troops, nor can the patients be too much divided. In general, diseases of a simple character get well in a few days if they are treated at once. They become aggravated if the patients have to be transported to a great distance; and the long return journeys, after recovery, exhaust men who are still weak and cause relapses that another journey may render fatal. Thus by multiplying hospitals and rendering them accessible to troops, we promote recovery, prevent diseases becoming aggravated, and patients being weakened; and we avoid the inconvenience caused by those contagious diseases so often the cause of the greatest ravages.

By this system more money is apparently spent, but the result is actually a great economy.

This is the system I have always pursued, and the troops under my charge have always flourished under it.

CHAPTER 5

On Military Justice, and on the Composition of the Tribunals

The social state cannot subsist if the conditions of its existence are not fulfilled. This is true of an army which offers the example of a private society, subject to special rules and manners. In order to discover the principle capable of solving our question, I inquire first what characterizes military justice, and I find that it is the complement of the means of discipline. To whose hands ought it to be confided? To the hands of those who are charged with the maintenance of discipline, who every day feel the need of it, perform its duties, and are those most interested in it Therefore it is the officers on active service to whom alone this care should be entrusted.

However, it was not always thus; during the revolution there were created military judges, civilians who accompanied the army. The error of such appointments was soon perceived; the consequences were disastrous, and courts-martial were established such as those of the present day.

In 1829, an endeavour was made to make a reform in this matter, and a new law on military justice was presented to the Chamber of Peers.

A commission, composed of men of eminence, but unacquainted with military affairs, proposed to substitute for the temporary courts-martial permanent military tribunals, presided over by general officers. This novel plan, by establishing a military magistracy distinct from the army, properly so called, would have had all the inconveniences of the system temporarily adopted under the republic, and would moreover have degraded in the eyes of the troops the character of the generals, who are essentially fighting men, and who ought by their presence to excite ideas of glory and reward, and not thoughts of crime and punishment.

Military justice is not established in an absolute way on principles of morality, it has necessity for its basis.

Doubtless in the eyes of every sensible man, in the point of view of morality and the protection of the person, there is a great difference between a thief and a soldier who disobeys and insults his chief in a moment of passion. And yet the punishment of the soldier is much more severe; for the satisfaction of society it is sufficient in many cases to send the former to the galleys, whereas the army would be ruined if the latter were not put to death; for, were he not, from that moment all the bonds of authority would be loosened, and the military edifice, whose foundations are respect and submission, would tumble to pieces without this support.

There is thus a great difference betwixt civil and military justice. The latter appears barbarous, but it is indispensable, and its execution can only be guaranteed by those whose very existence depends on it

As the battalion forms the fighting unit for the troops, the regiment forms the social military unit, the family and the tribe. The colonel, the head of this society, is invested with a sort of magisterial function which should watch over its preservation.

In him is vested the power to punish; it is his place to secure fox each prompt and impartial justice, to preserve order day by day, and see to the execution of the laws on which this order reposes. So when regular armies were first formed, each regiment had its own tribunal under the presidency of its colonel, and even at that time it was not only a necessity but a right, for each colonel, being the contractor of his regiment, required extensive legal powers in order to secure the obedience of his subordinates.

Regimental tribunals still exist in many of the great armies of Europe. Immediately available for the trial of offenders, their action can always be felt without delay. This consideration is of such immense importance, that this system is probably preferable to that adopted in France and Russia, of tribunals established by divisions only.

The motive that has influenced the legislator is easily understood; he wished to protect the accused from the personal passions of their chiefs by letting them be tried by a tribunal composed principally of officers strangers to their regiments. On the other hand these officers, being in active service and employed among the troops, it is certain that their judgment, given without prejudice, would be as severe as the welfare of the service required, for the presiding colonel would do in the interest of another regiment what would hereafter be done by another colonel for his own regiment; the welfare of the army would always be held in view.

In every court-martial there is a representative of each rank. This is a tribute paid to the feeling of duty which is observable equally in all degrees of the military hierarchy, and it is a guarantee for the accused, who have thus one or more of their equals among the judges. This arrangement is attended with no danger; for indulgence, were it to be dreaded, is much more likely to be found among the superior than the inferior ranks.

In conclusion, this I would remark, that for every reason military tribunals should be composed exclusively of individuals in active service, and belonging to the corps placed under their jurisdiction.

Another arrangement would perhaps be desirable in military justice; it exists in the Austrian army, and seems to me to be attended with salutary results. The right of pardon, and of commutation of sentence, is not the prerogative of the Sovereign, but of the proprietary colonel of the regiment, who usually delegates it to the colonel commanding. There are so many circumstances that may militate in favour of a soldier guilty of insubordination (it is generally for faults of that character that pardon is granted), the chiefs on the spot are so favourably placed for judging of the advisability or not of an act of clemency, that I believe it would be advantageous to give this prerogative, not to the colonel, but to the general commanding the division or the *corps d'armée*.

In the present state of affairs, a brave soldier, whose life all are anxious to save, is sacrificed to the rigour of the law; or, in order to save him, there is a denial of justice—two equally disagreeable alternatives.

CHAPTER 1

On the Employment of the Different Arms

The troops of the different arms should be separately organised, in order to receive the uniform instruction proper to each, and to be animated by a suitable spirit.

This principle has sometimes been neglected in the formation of *legions*, but never with good results. The officers in command of these corps, being best acquainted with the arm in which they have originally served, always give it the preference and devote most attention to it. Thus it would be absolutely impossible to provide for the instruction required by the artillery, without multiplying infinitely the necessary establishments such as the practice ground, the schools and batteries of all kinds. In fact, the artillery should be all united in one garrison if possible, in order that all may receive the same instruction. Were that so, the government could devote more money to this object, since a larger number of individuals would be instructed. I promised this when at the head of the French Artillery, but considerations of administration and economy, supported by local interests, prevented the adoption of this change.

But if in time of peace the various arms should be separated in order to carry out the special instruction required by each, in time of war they should be combined.

It is by their judicious and skilful admixture that the best results are obtained; they mutually support each other and act in concert. By keeping together the same corps during several campaigns under the same commander, an *esprit de corps* is created and thereby a useful homogeneity. Thus troops acquire their highest possible value. The legion of the Romans is the first instance of this combination which assuredly was a main cause of their triumphs. "A God," says Vegetius, "inspired them with the idea."

In the middle ages, in the succeeding times, and even up to our own days, the greatest generals never thought of imitating the Romans in this. Frederic the Great himself never thought of it. The first attempt was made in the French Army towards the end of the seven years war, under Marshal de Broglie, and to this general belongs the glory of giving practical effect to this profound thought But it never became an established plan until the commencement of the wars of the Republic. It is the greatest of the revolutions the art of war has undergone in modern times.

The infantry was formerly organised in brigades under the orders, when in formation, of two or three generals, one of whom commanded the centre and the others the wings. The cavalry was also divided and placed under the wings, and the subordinate commands were distributed for the day of battle. All the generals usually resided at headquarters, and were in turn entrusted with the command of detachments. If the general-in-chief wished to confide the temporary command of an expedition to a more able general or to one in whom he had more confidence than the one whose turn it was, he could not depart from the order of the list, so he was forced either to put off the operation, or to send out a number of detachments on fictitious errands, in order to employ all those whose turn came before the one he wished to employ.

The detachments being returned, the troops separated, and the brigades were assigned to their respective quarters by the officers of the staff. Under such a system, how could a large army move—get into formation and fight? Sometimes whole days were occupied in merely getting into order of battle. The smallest movement often caused confusion, and the artillery of position brought out of the park for the battle, and sometimes in battery the day before, was brought back to the park after action.

This barbarous and absurd system was altered during our first wars; and very soon all the European armies followed our example, by adopting the new organisation which renders the troops moveable and always ready to fight. In consequence, a commander had the means of easily making those combinations which circumstances demanded, and his genius suggested.

In the army, the fixed unit which should never vary, but whose strength may be greater or less, is the division. It is usually composed of two brigades,—each two, and sometimes three regiments strong; and of two batteries of artillery, and of a corps of mounted troops, 700 or 800 strong. It has its complete administration; it is, in fact, an army on a small scale. It may accordingly operate by its own resources: it may act independently: march, feed itself, and fight; or it may readily assume the part assigned to it on the day of battle.

It was in this way that the French Army was organised in the first immortal Italian campaign, and for several years afterwards. Later, Napoleon having formed *corps d'armée*, withdrew the cavalry from the divisions, and contented himself with applying to these *corps d'armée* the principles of the legion. But in the *corps d'armée*, the cavalry is too far from the divisions; it is not within reach of the fighting infantry generals: in many cases it is unable to take timely advantage of the disorders that occur among the enemy. By-and-bye I shall refer to the *corps d'armée*, and to the circumstances that authorised, indeed I may say, necessitated their formation.

The division is then the unit in the army, the primary element, by means of which the three arms are bound closely together; but this does not meet all the wants of an army.

Each arm, after having been accessory, should become in turn the principal, because there are circumstances in which it is desirable to produce a certain effect. Thus, reserves of cavalry are indispensable, either to fight masses of cavalry, or to be hurled against ill-supported bodies of infantry, or to cover infantry in disorder, or to storm batteries, &c.

This cavalry should be supported by an artillery belonging to it, and capable of assisting, according to circumstances, to attain the desired result. Here the cavalry is the principal and the artillery accessory. But the turn of the latter comes during the battle; the reserve artillery, employed to produce a great effect at a given moment and at a certain point, becomes all at once the principal arm, it crushes the enemy with its fire; then comes the infantry, which completes the disorder; and the cavalry finishes the work of destruction and ensures the victory.

I shall not enter into details, to show what are the circumstances in which artillery is called on to play its part alone, but I have said enough to prove that each arm should be in its turn accessory and principal; and if the artillery is intended to act on an isolated point, the infantry and cavalry destined to protect it, and to ensure its safety, should be subordinated to it in all the movements.

But the cavalry reserves, important as they are, should not be above a certain strength on a given point; beyond certain limits, the ablest commander cannot manage them; and moreover, too many horses assembled together cannot find the means of subsistence.

I reckon 6,000 mounted troops to be the outside number capable of being managed; with this number we should be able to succeed in all that is reasonable to attempt on the field of battle with cavalry.

Napoleon, in his latter campaigns, organised corps of cavalry composed of three divisions, amounting to at least 12,000 men. This was a monstrous idea, without any useful application on the battlefield; it was the cause of immense losses without fighting. These large bodies of mounted troops were never good for anything but to make an extraordinary show, and strike spectators with astonishment.

The organisation of armies demands divisions, and reserves of each arm. I allude to armies of moderate strength, for large armies require, in addition, another element of order and of action. This is obtained by forming the troops into *corps d'armée*; that is to say, that it is requisite to establish fixed commands, intermediate between the commander-in-chief and the generals of divisions.

An army of 100,000, composed of ten or twelve divisions, would be difficult to manage were it not organised into *corps d'armée*; for confusion would soon result from the excessive number of independent units, able to manoeuvre freely in obedience to a general direction given by the commander-in-chief. Hence the need of forming aggregations of divisions, in order to simplify the dispositions of the commander-in-chief was soon felt; and, two, three, or four divisions were joined together. Thus, an army composed as I have indicated is parted into four fractions, the commander-in-chief can move them easily, he has at his disposition four corps, three of which form his line of battle, and the fourth his reserve.

In all degrees of the military hierarchy, the exercise of the command is facilitated in proportion to the smallness of the number of immediate subordinates the chief has to deal with. The *corps d'armée* being small armies should have an organisation conformably to the principles I have established, and be composed—

1st. Of three divisions, in which the various arms are combined;
2nd. Of a cavalry reserve, supported by horse artillery;
3rd. Of an artillery reserve.

The reserves, which are meant to be sent in all directions, ought to be very *mobile*; and the artillery reserve, which has often to take post at great distances, should be mounted artillery.

Thus the ordinary artillery, which is organised so as to be extremely *mobile*, will serve along with the infantry divisions, and the horse artillery will be attached exclusively to the service of the cavalry and of the reserves.

The organisation which I have described is suited for the existing armies; it is the necessary consequence of the nature of the arms and of the mode in which war is now-a-days made; and the fractional parts into which the army is divided are designed to facilitate the exercise of the command. But there are various kinds of command, and they change their character according to the number of soldiers.

If a general fights with 10,000 men, he ought to be in the midst of his troops, and often exposed to the fire of small arms.

If a general is in command of 30,000 men, he directs the movements of his troops and reserves, and though he is usually, except in extraordinary cases, beyond the range of musketry, he must be constantly within that of cannon, and he must remain within the space where the balls fell.

If a general directs 80,000 or 100,000 men, he fixes the plan, and gives his orders before the battle; sets the troops in movement, and awaits the issue of events in a central position. During the action he becomes a kind of providence: he is ready with instructions for unforeseen cases, and he provides remedies for great accidents. He ought to expose himself before the battle, in order to see for himself, and to judge with precision of the state of things; having fulfilled these duties, he gives his orders, and lets each play the part assigned to him. If things go well, he has nothing else to do; if accidents occur, he should meet them by combinations within his power; if things go very badly, and a catastrophe is imminent, he should place himself at the head of the last troops that he launches against the enemy, and his presence at that momentous period, will give them an impulse and produce a moral effect that will double their value.

It was after this fashion that Napoleon commanded. As his operations were almost always crowned with success, and the armies he commanded very large, he rarely exposed himself to immediate danger. But at Lutzen, there having arisen a great crisis, which was very perilous from the nature of the army, composed as it was of young soldiers, he rallied his troops in person before Kaya, and led them to the charge under a murderous fire.

From what I have said above, the principles which have served as the basis for the creation of ranks, are apparent. It has been endeavoured to assimilate them to the natural commands, so that a general should have a well marked social position as regards his subordinates, always superior to them, even when not engaged in actual service.

France is the only country where, to the great detriment of the service, there exists no intermediate grade between those of lieutenant-general and marshal, for the command of *corps d'armée*. The dignity of marshal is suited only for a commander-in-chief, and sad experience has taught that several marshals in one army, acting under the orders of one of them, almost always occasion great misfortunes, in consequence of the disagreement and insubordination prevailing among them. It required an emperor, a great soldier himself, to command an army, the large portions of which were entrusted to marshals. It is true that corps were often under the orders of lieutenant-generals, to whom the temporary title of general-in-chief was given, and who received a commission to command. I should also add that anyone who had been so employed once was never afterwards appointed to the command of a simple division. But the grade being always the same, it is inconvenient to establish such relations voluntarily and without necessity.

As authority, necessary in all the relations of life, is supremely necessary among troops, and as it is essential that the chiefs, from him who commands an army, down to him who commands a company, should be replaced as soon as they disappear, it was requisite to establish as a principle the right of seniority to the command. But the accidental exercise of this right by the fortuitous result of the accidents of wars (all must be convinced of its necessity here) is a very different thing from the delegation of superior authority, without change of rank by the will of the sovereign when he is free to choose as he lists.

It offends one's self-esteem to have to obey one's equal, more especially if he is one's junior; and self-love, the cause of so much good and so much evil, has immense sway in the profession of arms, is in feet its very life.

An army composed of men destitute of self-esteem would be worthless; it is because they are fall of it that the French are each good soldiers; and it is thus that soldiers drawn from large towns, where self-esteem is more active, though they are inferior in strength and health, are often greatly superior in valour to those obtained from rural districts.

CHAPTER 2

On Offensive and Defensive Wars

I have said before, and I repeat it, that the movements in war, be it offensive or defensive, ought always to be based upon a calculation of time and distance. But the applications of this principle are easier in defensive than in offensive war.

In the latter the combinations are vaster, the conditions more variable, the elements of the calculation more uncertain. At each moment we may be forced to change parts, to abandon an attack in order to defend ourselves and escape great perils. It requires accordingly greater genius in order to be always ready to vary our designs and execute new combinations.

In defensive war, the theatre is more restricted; we operate on known ground, the nature of which we can appreciate exactly. The combinations being fewer in number it is easier to arrange and to prepare them. In offensive war genius must supply the place of experience and must guess at the nature of the country we are about to operate in: the points of supports on which we rely vary and sometimes disappear altogether. In defensive war we act on ground prepared and studied; we have fixed pivots of operation, everything may be calculated on with precision. Superior genius is therefore more necessary for offensive war, whilst great professional knowledge, a talent for selecting judiciously our points of support, extreme foresight, and indefatigable activity may suffice for the wants of defensive war.

Still this war is far from being easy, and all the more because properly speaking one is not reduced to act on the defensive unless the means at one's disposal are inferior to those of the enemy. Now, in modern warfare, supposing an equality of arms of instruction and of experience, numbers go for much. The difference betwixt one army and another in any one campaign, depends chiefly on the morale; and here the appreciation is not influenced by professional rules, but by that sublime part of the art which implies a knowledge of the human heart, the movements of which are so rapid and so mysterious.

After having stated the principle that should govern the movements of armies, it can only be developed by examples. Instruction is to be found in the study of the most remarkable campaigns. Dogmatic teaching rests on facts. We may select for this purpose reverses as well as successes, describing in the recital of each event the combination and accidents that distinguished it.

The preference should be given to the events of our own time for study; the examples will be better understood, the circumstances better known. Moreover, with the progress made by the art of war, with the actual and ever-increasing mobility of armies, that which was formerly impossible is now-a-days easy.

The wars of former times which may still be studied with advantage are those of Frederick II. It is true that the examples of that time are not at all applicable to the present day, so many changes having taken place; but it is in reference to the moral aspects of war, that this great captain deserves to be studied. When we see Frederick beaten at Hochkirchen with the loss of 200 guns, merely fall back two leagues on the Spree, take up position there, and brave the menaces of his victorious enemy, we ask in vain for a solution of a mystery which no one now-a-days can understand

When we consider the weakness of Frederick's resources, we are compelled to ask how it was that in the presence of such numerous enemies and during so many years he was able to support and to recruit his armies? Of a truth, we know not which to admire most, his victories or his fertility in resources and in his power of maintaining himself.

The long wars of our times, the great events which they offer for our consideration, all the circumstances attending which we ought to weigh well, deserve to be studied in the armies of the enemy as well as in our own.

The first campaign of the revolution presents nothing, either on our own side, or that of our adversaries, but what is deserving of censure, as we may convince ourselves by reading the first volume of the Memoirs of Marshal Gouvion Saint-Cyr, which in this respect is fraught with great interest.

The operations of the Archduke Charles in 1796, confronting the French armies of the Sambre and Meuse, and of the Rhine, are the first example of operations systematically combined on a large scale; accordingly we cannot bestow too much study on the work of this prince, where his principles are established with a frill account of the operations, and of the motives that guided them. All the great principles of war are there laid down, whilst they find their application in the facts there recorded.

But the campaigns that demand the greatest study are those of the French Army in Italy in 1796 and 1797. In them we find the greatest exactitude in the calculations, correctness in the movements, together with a profound acquaintance with men and things.

There never was such an admirable, such a perfect war. It is art in action in the most sublime manner. With moderate means immense results were obtained.

This war, that scarcely lasted a year, offers models of every description; offensive operations ably and audaciously conducted; defensive operations where inferior forces invariably repulsed superior forces, often securing the superiority of numbers on the field of battle; a war which, by the ability of its direction and the vigour of its execution, brought about an unexampled series of victories. It was in truth an immortal epoch when prodigies were performed surpassing anything that has ever been done before or since; for throughout that long series of combats, in the midst of so many and various movements it is impossible to detect a single fault—a single instance of forgetfulness of the true principles of the art.

At the opening of the campaign, the French Army, scarcely 30,000 strong, destitute of everything, had not completed its preparations when it was forced to commence operations, as the enemy was marching on Genoa, in order to cover that stronghold. The enemy's army, more than 60,000 strong, but composed of troops of two different nations, was attacked. The Austrians were beaten, pursued, and very soon held in check by a single division. The French army threw itself on the Piedmontese: complete and rapid success spread confusion and discouragement among the Allies, and the King of Sardinia made peace.

By a forced march the French Army surprised the passage of the Po, which, from want of means, it would have been unable to cross in the face of an enemy. By an energetic effort it crossed the Adda. Milan opened its gates. Shortly afterwards an entire province was in insurrection; the insurrection was repressed. The army, which had scarcely slackened its march for an instant, forced the passage of the Mincio, gained the Adige, and took up a defensive position, covering the conquests made in less than 50 days. The enemy formed successive armies, which made impotent attacks on ours. Mantua fell; we marched on Vienna, and peace was concluded.

Nothing could be more useful for the instruction of officers who desire to devote themselves to the study of war on a grand scale, and of military conceptions of a superior order, than a work on this memorably campaign, giving the details and the documents connected with it. To these should be added commentaries explaining the reasons for the various movements, showing their spirit and their results. The campaign of 1805, so brilliant, so well conducted, and so remarkable in its issue, favoured, it is true, by the immense and almost incredible faults of our adversaries; that of 1806, which completes it, and lastly, that of 1809, might be the subject of a special study, and of instructive commentaries; for it is impossible to admire too much this grand period of Napoleon's career.

But we must pass over in silence the wars of the Spanish Peninsula, and of the subsequent period, or at least mention them only to point out their faults, and to show that Napoleon deserved to be forsaken by fortune when he proved faithless to the true principles of war, which up to that time he had always respected. This accumulation of men and of means was useless. Dating from that period of sad memory, except at Lutzen and Bautzen, we no longer recognise Napoleon in any of his campaigns.

However, a sort of revival occurred later. The great captain was himself again in 1814; but opinion only fought for him there; he had no longer an army. We were scarcely one to ten. In his movements betwixt the Seine and the Marne, Napoleon never had at his command more than a fragmentary force of 35,000 men. My corps, which had the sole glory of the combats of Champ-Aubert, Vauchamps, Montmirail, and the second affair at Gué-à-Trême, never amounted to 4,000 men, the remains of 52 different battalions. At Paris, supported by the Duke of Treviso, our united forces numbered 14,000 men, whilst the enemy had 53,000 men engaged, and 13,000 killed and wounded. It was the swan's dying song.

CHAPTER 3

On Marches and Encampment

Too great precaution cannot be exercised in marches within reach of the enemy, nor too much prudence displayed in forming encampments. Everyone knows how the former are performed; but we should modify, according to the nature of the country, the composition of the advanced guards and the relative position of the arms of which they are composed.

The object being to get information respecting the enemy, and to be aware of his approach, it is advantageous to reconnoitre to as great a distance as possible, taking care, however, not to compromise the safety of our detachments. The vanguard of an army, not in presence of the enemy, should be at least a good day's march away from the main body of the troops, and that of a division several hours in advance.

Light troops should be employed intelligently, and should not be spared, for it is especially in this service that they are useful if they allow the army to be surprised their commander has failed to do his duty. He can offer no good excuse for his neglect. In broken and wooded countries our precautions must be redoubled. The scouts thrown out on the flanks should be supported by detachments whose business it is to collect them; and these detachments should be strong enough to defend, for some time, any defiles that might allow the enemy to turn our army.

If we arrange the march of troops sent to reconnoitre so that they shall be in the form of a fan, we shall secure ourselves from anything like a surprise; and we shall not expose the troops, because their point of retreat is always on the line of operation of the army.

On the march, encampments are made in order to rest the troops and to satisfy their wants, but not for fighting purposes. The best position for an encampment is the banks of a stream, because the soldiers have there abundance of water at their disposal, and the resources of a concentrated population. But, important as are these considerations, security must also be attended to, and we must not neglect the means of resisting an unforeseen attack and a surprise. I do not allude to the guards which ought always to cover and envelop the camp; they are absolutely necessary, were it only as police.

When there is an obstacle the site of the camp should be chosen on the nether, and never on the further side of it; at least, as far as regards the greater part of the troops. No doubt it would be advantageous, on commencing to march the following day, to have passed a defile so as to advance more easily; but this advantage is fully compensated by being able to rest in security. If there is no obstacle, or only such an obstacle as may be easily turned, a surprise is to be apprehended. A numerous body of cavalry may suddenly appear as if sprung out of the ground. In such a case security would have to be obtained from the disposition of the camp itself.

There are two modes of encamping; one by deploying the troops, the other by forming them in a mass by battalions. This latter disposition is by much the preferable one, and offers all sorts of advantages. It is executed as follows:—

A division is placed on two lines, and each battalion is formed in mass by grand divisions; it is separated into two demi-battalions in mass by companies. The interval that separates the two fractions is equal to the front of a grand division, and forms a road at right angles to the line of battle of the camp.

The tents or huts are established on the right and left, and their doors are made to open on the road, either directly or by means of a transverse lane. When the battalion is called to arms, each soldier goes to his company, which assembles in the road of the camp, and the battalion is at once formed and ready to march. If the impetuosity of a large body of cavalry is such that it precipitates itself upon the camp, it will find all the troops in a mass, and, as it were, entrenched in the midst of their tents and huts.

Neglect of the above rules was the cause of a great disaster on the 29th of May, 1813, near Haynau in Silesia. The division Maison, which had marched all day long, and taken up a position without reconnoitring sufficiently, was surprised; twenty-two squadrons of Prussian cavalry, lying in ambush in the neighbouring forest, sallied forth unexpectedly just when the division was settling itself down; it was almost totally destroyed without having been able to fight.

On another occasion, similar negligence on the part of the Prussians enabled us to have our revenge and gain an easy victory. After the Battle of Champ-Aubert (10th February, 1814), where my *corps d'armée* had by itself destroyed or taken almost the entire Russian corps of Olsufieff, the emperor ordered me to go to Etoges in order to cover the army on that side, whilst he marched on Montmirail, occupied by the corps of Sacken. Sacken having been beaten retreated on Chateau-Thierry, where he passed the Marne in order to stay the pursuit of Napoleon, who had followed him. During this time, Blücher in person advanced with the corps of Kleist and marched on Etoges; on the 13th he prepared to force us to evacuate this advantageous post, which I pretended I was going to defend, in order to delay Blücher's march.

I retreated; the enemy followed us closely, but with great circumspection, and up to the evening there had been only some slight skirmishing with light troops. I took my position on the skirts of the forest of Fromentière, and the enemy encamped at two cannon-shot distance from us. I had announced to Napoleon Blücher's arrival, and had told him of the movement I was going to make. I was certain of his speedy return. On the 14th, at 4 a.m., I set out in order to get near Montmirail, and I sent an officer to get tidings of the emperor. He had just arrived, and sent to tell me that I might attack the enemy when I thought fit, that he was prepared to support me.

In front of the village of Vauchamps, on the side next to Paris, there is an advantageous and easily defensible position; it is the slope of the *plateau* that forms the side of the valley in which Vauchamps is situated. On the right, a wood a little ahead enables one to take in reverse any enemy who should advance without taking the precaution of first making himself master of it. I caused this wood to be occupied quietly; I deployed my troops on the eminence; I placed my guns in battery, and we waited for the enemy.

Kleist's corps, four times the strength of mine, thought it had nothing to fear, and marched with the utmost confidence, its troops in close columns, and giving themselves no trouble about reconnoitring. Finding the village unoccupied, Kleist passed through it; but being assailed by a murderous fire of artillery, and attacked at once in front and on his flanks, his corps was thrown into confusion: it fled out of the village in the greatest disorder; and our cavalry falling upon it, we took 4,000 prisoners. From that moment the enemy, who was in no regular formation, retreated *en masse* until the evening, when this day so brilliant for us, terminated for him in a new catastrophe.

The victory of Hohenlinden, the glory and the results of which were so great, is an event of that nature. The column of the centre of the Austrian Army which pursued the main road, and to which had been joined a large part of the artillery of the lateral columns for the purpose of facilitating its transport, was in advance of the other columns, and it marched without taking sufficient care to reconnoitre, owing to the confidence inspired in it by the battle of the previous day, and under the belief that the French army was in fall retreat. It encountered the latter in the very middle of the forest. Being vigorously attacked before it was able to make the necessary dispositions for resisting, soon taken in flank, this immense column of material was carried off, and the battle gained.

There is no more delicate operation, nor any which requires more care than to march across a much wooded country with a numerous artillery, in presence of the enemy. Desirous though we may be to meet him, we cannot, under such circumstances, take too many precautions to prevent ourselves being surprised, for the consequences of the slightest negligence are almost always disastrous.

On the 29th of August, 1813, after the Battle of Dresden, I was ordered to pursue the enemy's army, the greater part of which was retreating by the Attenberg road. Having beaten at Possendorf and at Dippodiswalda the corps which covered the movement of concentration, my intention was to continue the following day my march on Falkenheim. On my arrival at the village of Frauendorf, I learned that the enemy occupied a good position at Falkenheim, with a strong advanced guard. Before plunging into the forest I had to traverse, which was occupied by some light troops, I caused it to be cleared by 3,000 or 4,000 infantry soldiers extended over a large space. Having thus freed it from the enemy, I took up my position on the skirts of the wood with my advanced guard, and waited till my whole corps joined me. I then rushed out of the forest with all my forces; in a moment the enemy was overthrown and chased from his position, leaving behind almost all his artillery.

There are also marches executed in presence of the enemy with a complete army in battle array, and ready to fight, with the design of making the enemy quit a position occupied by him. Such marches belong to the movements of tactics; nothing deserves more care, nor requires more precautions.

In order to execute a movement of this character, we must have troops highly disciplined, and accustomed to manoeuvre, vigilant and active generals, and a commander endowed with great foresight.

The Army of Portugal, in 1812, under my command, made such a march successfully.

The French and English armies were encamped on both sides of the Douro; the former was inferior to the latter by 6,000 infantry and 4,000 cavalry. In spite of the disproportion of the forces, I had to take the offensive. I was informed by my official correspondence that I should not receive any important support; and on the other hand, the English Army, which was already superior, could get powerful reinforcements in a few days from Estremadura, by the bridge of Alcantara, whilst the army of Gallicia, which blockaded Astorga, was about to become free to operate on my rear owing to the surrender of the town, which, through want of food, was about to open its gates. I came to the conclusion that in order to change the state of affairs it was necessary I should assume the offensive, but with prudence, to manoeuvre in order to force the enemy to retreat, and not to fight unless it was unavoidable. The passage of the Douro was then resolved and executed.

The French Army, all assembled, encountered next day two English divisions at Tordesillas-de-la-Orden, which hastily retired. They were closely pursued, and would probably have been destroyed in consequence of their isolation, if the French cavalry had not been so inferior to that of the enemy.

The two armies found themselves face to face the evening of the pursuit, and separated by the Guarena, a marshy brook.

The 20th of July, the French Army, all formed in order of battle, broken into companies, made a flanking manoeuvre by its left in order to ascend the brook; on gaining a passage previously reconnoitred and quickly improved, it got its advance over the left bank, took possession of the slopes of a plateau, which extends indefinitely in a direction that threatened to cut off the retreat of the enemy, and then the army advanced under the protection of a large battery which covered its movements.

The Duke of Wellington thought at first that he would be able to oppose this offensive march; but it was executed so rapidly and in such order, that he soon gave up the idea of attacking us.[1] He then set the English Army in motion and marched along, a plateau parallel to that

---

1. The Duke of Wellington afterwards told me that the French Army marched "like one regiment." That was his expression.

occupied by us.

The two armies continued their marches, separated by a narrow valley, always in readiness to accept battle. Several hundreds of cannon shot were exchanged when the sinuosities of the plateau allowed it; for both generals desired to accept, not to give battle. After a march of five leagues performed in this manner, they arrived at the respective positions they wished to occupy, the French Army on the heights of Aldea-Rubia, the English Army on those of Saint Cristoval.

This remarkable march is, as fax as I know, the only one performed in our own times. But it may be repeated in a war where the forces are nearly equal, and when the commanders are unwilling to fight unless with assured advantages, and under certain very favourable circumstances.

CHAPTER 4

On Reconnaissances in Force and On the Precautions They Require

To know the position of the enemy, to have timely information of the movements he executes, to collect sufficient data in order to divine his projects,—these are among the greatest difficulties devolving on the command of an army. Nothing should be neglected in order to obtain exact information, and the surest means is to be constantly in contact with the enemy by means of light troops, to have frequent skirmishes, and to take prisoners whose replies to queries are almost always frank and sincere. More is to be learned from them than from the most trustworthy spies; the latter often confound the names of corps and generals and form very incorrect estimates of the strength of the troops they report upon.

When two armies, by the combinations of war, are brought suddenly into the presence of, or have remained long at a certain distance from each other, it is well to assure ourselves more positively of the situation of affairs; we then execute what are called *reconnaissances in force*. These operations demand much prudence, and even a particular foresight, unless under extraordinary and very advantageous conditions.

We must employ in them a strong force of cavalry, and we should, if possible, let no troops be engaged but cavalier and horse artillery, in order to have more command over our movements. Our object is to tear aside the veil that conceals the enemy, and if the commander is able to advance far enough to see with his own eyes the situation of the enemy, he has attained his object.

But he should hold himself in readiness to support the troops he has caused to be engaged, and to rally them if they have been repulsed too hotly. He should have at hand a considerable body of infantry; and behind them the army should be so disposed that it should be ready to march at once, if required, and take part in the action. An instant's delay may make us lose opportunities suddenly arising, which, if at once taken advantage of, would yield unforeseen advantages.

I shall adduce an instance where inattention to this precept prevented me from gaining an easy victory over the English army in Spain. More instruction is often to be gained by pointing out faults than relating successes.

In 1811 I occupied the valley of the Tagus with the Army of Portugal. My duty was to watch over the safety of two strongholds which covered the north and the south, Ciudad Rodrigo and Badajoz, which belonged to the armies of the south and north, and formed parts of their districts. Ciudad Rodrigo being in want of food. General Dorsenne, commanding the army of the north, organised a large convoy, and prepared to lead it. He provided it with an escort of 10,000 infantry and 2,000 cavalry. But the concurrent action of the army of Portugal was essential for the safety of its march, as the English army was not far off. I took the larger portion of the army beyond the pass of Bânos, and placed my army in *échelon* from Tamames to the river of Agueda.

I repaired to Rodrigo with 1,500 sabres. General Dorsenne came there also, and threw into the fortress a small division of 3,000 infantry, commanded by General Thiebault, with a large supply of food. The report was current that the English were preparing to make the siege of Rodrigo, and that they had collected large stores of supplies within reach. It was advisable to assure ourselves of this, and it was determined that a double *reconnaissance* in force should be made in the direction of the Almeida road, and upon the heights of Elbodon, where the English Army had its advanced posts. This reconnaissance was to be made by the cavalry of the army of Portugal under General Montbrun.

General Thiebault was ordered to support it, if necessary. The position of Elbodon was carried in an instant. The English cavalry put to flight, and a brigade of English infantry was isolated. After having courageously stood several charges it retreated on Fuente Guinaldo. Favoured by a difficult ground—and thanks to the quickness of its march and its valorous behaviour—it could not be routed. It was important to occupy, without delay, Fuente Guinaldo—a place where many roads meet, and a strategical point for the assembly of the army.

The division Thiebault was summoned; but it was too fax off, because it had only come out for the purpose of defence and safety, and the field of battle was extremely distant in consequence of the retreat of the enemy, so that it arrived too late, and its great weakness did not allow of its being hurled, at the beginning of the night, at the entrenchments of Fuente Guinaldo, towards which columns were approaching from different sides.

Had I had at hand 8,000 men I would have acted with confidence. Fuente Guinaldo would have fallen into my power. The light division placed at Martiago, on the right bank, would probably have been captured or destroyed; the English Army dispersed, and, its various corps being unconnected with one another, would have been placed in the most critical position. But, having time to reassemble, it hastily retreated; and the opportunity for obtaining an easy and complete success was missed.

I repeat, when we make a reconnaissance in force, we should always so dispose our troops that we shall not be forced to accept a serious engagement; but, at the same time, we should be in a condition either to rally the troops engaged, should they be beaten, or to profit, by some accidental and favourable circumstance. Whatever respect we may entertain for our opponent, we should not consider him infallible. Fortune often smiles on us when we least expect it; and we should always be prepared to show her that we are worthy of her favours.

CHAPTER 5

On Detachments in Presence of the Enemy, Their Suitableness, and the Dangers Attending Them

Sometimes a commander, too confident of the success he anticipates, makes all his dispositions for securing great results for the victory before he has beaten the enemy. With this object, he divides his forces and sends them in various directions; instead of being victorious he is beaten. The detachments he has sent out are taken prisoners or destroyed, and a campaign commenced under good auspices results in a series of reverses.

I shall adduce several instances in support of the truth of what I advance.

In 1796, in Italy, Wurmser opened the campaign with a larger army than that of the French; a column was sent round the latter by Brescia to destroy its communications. This column, too weak to resist the united French army, retired as the latter approached. Separated from the larger part of the army by the mountains and the Lago-di-Garda, it remained ignorant of the events that ensued; and the French Army, situated between the two, beat one after the other all the corps which successively came up against it.

In the same year, General Alvinzi debouched from the Tyrol and attacked the French Army occupying the chain of Mount Baldo and La Corona. Believing victory to be certain, he detached a corps of 5,000 men, commanded by Colonel Lusignan, which, after following the border of the Lago-di-Garda, changed its direction, approached the Adige, and took up a position in the rear of the French Army, and on its direct communications. This corps was held in check by the weak division Rey, which was connected with the main army, and

93

which took up a position fronting the hostile corps. The battle was gained by the French Army, and Lusignan's corps, being attacked and put to rout, was almost entirely captured.

In 1800, Napoleon entered Italy with an army of 60,000 men. Having crossed the Po and completely turned the Austrian Army, he came upon its communications and endeavoured to take possession of all the roads by which it might try to retire.[1] In order to do this, he placed a portion of his forces on the left bank of the Po, on the Ticino, whilst he was obliged to send a division on the Adda and the Oglio, so as to cover himself on that side. Then, supposing that the Austrian army assembled at Alessandria would retreat on Genoa, he detached a division in the direction of Novi to intercept the passage by that route. He retained beside him only 22,000 men, and the enemy had 45,000 assembled on the Bormida.

The enemy attacked; the Battle of Marengo was fought; obstinately contested, it seemed to be lost at 5 o'clock in the afternoon, when the division detached on Novi arrived. General Desaix, who commanded it, wisely arrested its march on hearing the sound of cannon, and waited for orders. It retraced its steps, and came just in time to act as a reserve, and the battle was gained, though only 27,000 men were able to take part in the fight; and of these, 22,000 had to support the whole weight of the battle. Thus our forces engaged were only two-thirds of those of the enemy, and it very nearly happened that they were only one-half. It was, no doubt, a brilliant victory, the consequences of which were immense; but it would be dangerous to take as a model the strategical combinations that brought it about, for it ought to have been lost, considering the superiority of the forces and means opposed to us.

Though victories arc possible under such circumstances, we should not reckon too much on them. No doubt we should display all the more energy the more unfavourable the circumstances are; but we should not wilfully seek to create such unpromising conditions.

In 1813 the French Army of Silesia—more than 80,000 strong—assembled at Goldsberg, under the command of the Marshal Duke of Tarento, was confronted by an army of almost equal strength, commanded by Blücher. The Duke of Tarento advanced upon the enemy,

---

1. Nothing remained of the array that fought at Marengo but the corps of Victor, formed of the two small divisions, Gardanne and Chambarlhac; the corps of Lannes, composed of the divisions Vatrin and Monier; the division Boudet, of 6,000 men; a very small force of cavalry; and 32 pieces of ordnance.

whom he believed to be assembled at Janer. Just as he was about to move, be detached the division Puthod, and sent it towards Janer by Schönau, in order to find the enemy and take him in flank.

But Blücher had at the same moment commenced an offensive movement The French Army, imperfectly informed, encountered the enemy unexpectedly, near Katzbach, and was obliged to accept battle before it could assemble its forces. Bad combinations, and a series of unlucky events, threw the army into confusion. The French Army being beaten, was forced to fall back. The division Puthod lost its communications; was driven to the Bober, which was flooded, and overpowered by numbers. After a gallant fight it was obliged to surrender.

From the examples cited, and from many others I could adduce, it follows:—

1st. That nothing is more hazardous than to make an important detachment before having fought, conquered, and thereby got a decided ascendancy over the enemy.

2nd. The execution of this dangerous combination demands that the army should have a sufficient superiority in order to ensure the greatest probability of victory, and we should never so weaken our main force as to make it inferior in strength to that we have to fight

3rd. When we are far from an enemy sufficiently strong to offer battle to us, and when marching towards him, we should occupy, with advanced guards and light troops, at least the space of a good day's march around us, in order to be informed of his movements, and modify our own accordingly,

4th. Lastly, when we deem it right to make an isolated detachment, we should determine its direction, and place troops to support it in such a manner that it shall always be able to fall back securely on the army, and shall in no case lose its communications.

CHAPTER 6

On Battles

It would be impossible to enter into full details respecting the dispositions required in the conduct of a battle; a thousand unforeseen circumstances may occur to modify them; fortuitous accidents suddenly arise to change all our plans. I shall confine myself to laying down the rules we must obey and the principles we must attend to in order to prepare the battle and distinguish its particular character. As to the mode of giving battle, nothing is more variable. It differs according to the nature of the operations to be executed, and the kind of mission the army has received. It varies with the composition of armies and the peculiar genius of the soldiers; it varies still more according to the talent and the kind of faculties of the generals commanding. I shall enter into very few technical details respecting the formation of the troops and their preliminary distribution, for these dispositions depend chiefly on the nature of the ground on which we have to fight.

Thus, for example, it is evident that any position near the field of battle which could serve as a shelter or support should be occupied in force and in such a way as to prove advantageous, whether we act on the offensive or the defensive. A strong position makes up for a deficiency of numbers; defiles on our front render a portion of the means of defence superfluous, and the means of attack more difficult The slightest reflection, often mere instinct, will suffice to make us aware of the modifications necessary to be made in the formations usually adopted.

I shall only state in a few words that apart from the influence of locality, the formations of troops on several lines has been adopted as a fundamental principle. The first deployed, the second in columns of battalions at deploying distance, ready, if necessary, to march or to place itself in battle array; and a third line comprising the reserve, in columns of brigades, ready to go whithersoever its services may be required.

I shall, therefore, make one observation respecting the general dispositions, *viz.*, that the commands of the troops should be divided so as to embrace the two lines at once,—that is to say, that the corresponding parts of each should be under the command of the same chief. The reason of this is obvious. As the second line is intended to support the first, it is requisite that the movements of the corresponding portions of the two lines should be in perfect accord. The same is not the case with the reserve; it forms a complete and independent corps, which should have all its means together in order to act according to circumstances; thus a *corps d'armée* of four divisions, in battle array, should, in my opinion, have the following formation :—

In the first line, three brigades of three different divisions, and in the second the three other brigades of the same division; and the fourth in the rear entire, and formed in two masses of one brigade each.

The cavalry should be placed thus:—that belonging to the divisions on the flank and in the rear of their respective divisions, and the masses of cavalry on several lines and on the flanks of the army, on a level with the second line, and by preference on the side where the country is most open and most favourable to its movements.

As to the artillery, that of the reserve should be in the rear of the infantry of the reserve, ready to go where it may be required.

In conclusion, I may add, that the art of directing a battle well consists particularly in the judicious and opportune employment of the reserves; and that the commander who in a well contested battle shall have fresh and disposable troops at the end of the day, after his adversary has used up all his, is nearly sure to be victorious.

As regards their character battles may be divided into two classes—defensive and offensive battles.

In regard to the first, the conditions of success are:—the choice of a good position, the flanks of which are well protected and the rear free and covered; the obstacles that render the approach of the enemy more difficult in his front; and, lastly, the troops brave, disciplined, and commanded by an energetic and resolute man.

Offensive battles require, above all, a good strategical combination and able tactics; troops well drilled, good marchers, active, intelligent, with a certain amount of impetuosity about them. The soldier should be ambitious of success as something appertaining to him, and he ought to count on obtaining it.

Applying these observations, which I believe to be quite correct, to the spirit of the different armies, and looking for illustrative examples among the troops most unlike one another, we become aware that the genius of the French troops is more for offensive, that of the English for defensive battles. If in addition we observe that in offensive war the difficulties of the administration and maintenance of troops are immense, whereas in defensive war all that is required is money and will; if we reflect, moreover, that the English Army by its composition, its habits, its wants, requires more than any other to be in the midst of abundance, we shall be all the more convinced that defensive war, with all its consequences, is more adapted to the faculties of an English Army, and that it would be conducted less easily by a French army.

The events of the Peninsular War, still fresh in our memory, vouch for the truth of the above. The English commander, whether owing to his nature and character, or to his ability to turn to the best account the circumstances in which he was placed, understood from the very commencement the system he ought to pursue, and never desisted from it.

For a long time he perseveringly availed himself of a powerful auxiliary which the force of circumstances favoured him with, our poverty; he worked this mine incessantly. His own army abundantly supplied with everything, able to assemble any day, was always able to move, was always threatening; military and political considerations alone influenced his operations, while the French Army, abandoned to penury of all sorts, forced to perform all kinds of duties, saw its means and strength daily diminish. If there was an impregnable position, the English general occupied it, and waited until it was threatened to be turned, or until the French army came and dashed itself against the insurmountable natural obstacles, wasting its valour without result.

Thus, when Marshal Massena at the head of a superior army threatened to invade Portugal, Wellington placed himself behind two fortified places, and being in addition covered by the Coa, he waited until the French Army had exhausted a portion of its means by two sieges; abandoning to the fortune of war the garrisons of these two strongholds which did not belong to his own army, he retired after their capitulation when he might have apprehended an attack on himself, and took up a position at Busaco; after having repulsed an ill-advised attack of the French Army, he made off and disappeared, when the latter attempted to turn him; and the English Army retired within the lines of Lisbon, where the powerful means of resistance offered by nature had been strengthened by art.

The English general waited patiently until famine and misery had disorganised the French Army; he pursued this system so strictly, that he refrained from attacking it, though it was within cannon-shot and incapable of accepting battle or offering any serious resistance, weakened as it was by the absence of 15,000 or 20,000 men, who, leaving their arms piled, ran off to the distance of 15 to 20 leagues in search of food in the interior of Portugal. Reduced to nearly one-half, the French army returned to Spain, after abandoning all its guns and all its material, owing to the want of horses to transport it, and three-fourths of its cavalry had to go on foot It suffered immense losses, though the only place where it fought was at Busaco, and during the retreat it had only two unimportant skirmishes.

Wellington always pursued a similar system: and when in after years he found himself opposed to Napoleon at Waterloo, he still acted on the defensive.

We see, then, that in defensive war, which is always an affair of time, battles should be fought as seldom as possible, for marches and various other circumstances sometimes injure and destroy the means of an adversary more certainly than would the most signal victory.

With regard to the particular circumstances of defensive battles, they should always be fought in front, and the great thing is to force the enemy by wisely conceived dispositions to attack at the point where resistance is easiest. But there are also battles which, beginning with an offensive movement, in the coarse of the action assume a defensive character; this happens when prudent and circumspect commanders at the head of nearly equal forces wish the battle to commence.

In 1812 there occurred an example of this: the English Army was stronger than the French by 8,000 infantry and 4,000 cavalry. The French general, after having long acted on the defensive in the expectation of additional troops which had been promised, having been officially informed that they would not be sent, was obliged to assume the offensive in order to prevent his situation becoming daily worse.

But in assuming the offensive and forcing the enemy to retreat by strategical movements, though he was resolved to fight, he did not wish by an ill-considered attack to have a repetition of the events that had previously occurred. He desired if a battle were to take place that it should be fought on ground of his choice, that it should be accepted, not given, by himself. On the other hand the English general, faithful to his system, also resolved to reduce the action to the defence of a position. Hence the remarkable movements that took place from the Douro to the Tonnes towards the middle of the month of July, 1812.

Both parties acting on this plan, the English Army was obliged to make a retrograde march. The immediate result of this part of the campaign would undoubtedly have been its retreat upon the Agueda, and its return to Portugal, had it not been for a movement executed without orders in the French Army, and had not the marshal commanding it received a serious wound three quarters of an hour before the battle commenced; the result was a degree of uncertainty in the command preventing the faults committed being repaired in time, and bringing on a general action that should not have been commenced until a later period and under better auspices. In spite of these disadvantages the losses of both armies were equal.

Though I am firmly persuaded that French troops, well commanded and adequately provided, are suitable for all kinds of warfare, I yet believe that offensive war is more adapted to the spirit, the nature and the character of our soldiers; it was especially suited to the genius of Napoleon.

I have already said that no one ever possessed a higher degree of strategical ability than himself, and his offensive marches up to the period of the Russian war were ably conceived. The immense forces at his disposal, their energy, the spirit that animated them, his activity, the absolute liberty he enjoyed in forming his projects and combinations, hurried on events, and whilst they encouraged his own soldiers they produced a discouraging effect beforehand on the enemy; and those who dread being beaten are not very far from being defeated. Besides, what a succession of brilliant operations, executed in a magical manner!

At the commencement of his career, in Italy, he turned every position, and beat the enemy in detail, before he was able to unite his forces. He passed the Po without having an enemy before him, because he outstripped them in his movements. The war became a defensive one, but he soon changed its character, and by attacking he again assumed the part most suited to his genius.

In 1800 he entered Italy and forced the Austrian Army to accept battle in the most disastrous position, under the most disadvantageous conditions, after it had lost its communications and its point of retreat.

In 1805 the mere direction of his armies, which he marched in a mass towards the Danube, after having displayed some heads of columns in the Black Forest, in order to distract the enemy's attention, decided the question of the campaign; for if Mack, in place of having accelerated the catastrophe of the Austrian army by his insane confidence, had retired, this simple movement would have given us possession of all Bavaria.

At Austerlitz it was a tactical movement that, in a few hours, decided the fate of the battle. At Jena the same prodigies were performed by the same means. As long as he followed this system, all Napoleon's enterprises were crowned by a like success.

In 1809, at the outset of the campaign, it was the same spirit that guided his operations. But he soon changed his system; after having failed once to cross the Danube, he succeeded on a second attempt, and gained a battle in the plains of Wagram. There it was an attack in front—a direct attack that won the battle. Indeed, the circumstances of the case left him no choice in the matter. The passage of a river like the Danube is no easy matter, and cannot be performed by surprise; and if an army placed on the opposite bank is seriously disposed to dispute it, we must make up our minds to fight on getting over; in that case, superiority of means and energy can alone give the victory.

In 1812, it was in his option to give to the grand battle he fought on the Moskowa the character of his previous victories; a simple flanking movement would have enabled him to fight the Russian Army to much greater advantage, and promised much greater results. But already he had commenced to exhibit a marked preference for direct attacks, for the employment of sheer strength, and a certain contempt for the assistance of art and combinations requiring mental effort. He gained the victory, but at the cost of immense losses and with insignificant advantages.

In 1813 he varied his method.

At Lutzen, having been surprised, the battle commenced by being defensive, but it was soon changed into offensive. At Bautzen the strategical combinations were ably conceived. But at Leipsic we cannot understand why Napoleon, who might have changed the theatre of operations, should voluntarily choose such a disadvantageous one, which the simplest calculations might have shown him would be disastrous to himself. The battle of the 18th October was defensive and offered no chance of success, because the battle of the 16th had not

101

been won, and because the enemy had on the 17th received reinforcements to the extent of 150,000 men. He should have declined the battle and retired without delay.

In France the battles of Brienne, of Craon, of Laon, and of Arcis could not be of any advantage, in consequence either of the concentration of the forces, or of the direction of the attacks; all the operations of that period should have been limited to partial movements directed against separated bodies of the enemy. It was in such operations only that what remained of energy in the French army should have been expended; such combinations, moreover, were suited to the genius of Napoleon, and he had already employed them several times successfully at Champ-Aubert, at Montmirail, at Vauchamp, and at Montreau, giving to an obstinate defensive war an offensive character which was best adapted to his talents.

But being at length reduced to the necessity of fighting by the junction of all the forces of the enemy, he ought to have fought a defensive battle, to have selected a position near Paris, fortified it, then drawn thither all his means and those of the capital which he alone could command, and in that position he should have tried his fortune for the last time.

If a remnant of 14,000 men, abandoned to their own resources in an open country, without a single field-work to support them, deprived of the aid which the city might have furnished them in consequence of the disappearance and flight of the superior authorities, could for ten hours offer effective resistance to the enormous forces opposed to them, 60,000 of whom were engaged and 13,000 put *hors de combat*, it is easy to calculate what could and should have happened if 30,000 men had fought, protected by well made works that would have tripled their strength, and aided by all the means Paris could afford, which would have been secured to them by the presence and the authority of Napoleon.

But this kind of resolution was not in his genius; he would neither foresee it nor make any preparations to put it in execution; he relied on public opinion only as the last lever of his power. And yet though the force of opinion is immense, it has no durability unless based on something positive and real.

One more word respecting offensive battles. At what hour of the day should they be fought? This is a question worth examining, as it is of great importance.

When we have our choice we should vary the hours according to circumstances. If we possess such a decided superiority as to authorise a firm confidence in victory, we should attack early in the morning, in order to be able to profit by the success obtained. No soldier can forget the vexations he has experienced on seeing night approach when successful, and the impatience with which he has looked for it when defeated.

The attack should also be made as early as possible when we have all our troops in hand, whereas the enemy has not yet assembled all his. It has been repeatedly asked why Napoleon at Waterloo, on one of the longest days of the year, delayed his attack on the English till eleven o'clock a.m., although he knew from an interrupted dispatch of Blücher to Wellington, that the Prussian commander would not be able to come up before four o'clock p.m.? for had Napoleon commenced early, if victorious he would confront the Prussians after having beaten the English, or if he had been worsted, he would at least have avoided having to do with a second army in the middle of the battle.

Great military questions may almost always be reduced to simple ideas, and here the formula is that we have more chance of success in fighting one against one than one against two.

But a near equality of forces making victory uncertain, it is better to attack about the middle of the day; the consequences of a defeat are less formidable, and a general ought before all things to think of the preservation of his army. The destruction of the enemy is only a secondary consideration in the order of duties and interests. Besides, if the issue of the battle is undecided, we have all the night to prepare for a new attack and fresh combinations. Then, again, the troops are more rested, they have been able to have a meal before the battle, they are full of strength and energy. On the other hand, the army that is acting on the defensive being agitated by apprehensions of attack, cannot indulge in such perfect repose, and often become depressed in courage as the moment of action approaches.

In the midst of our Italian triumphs, two small reverses occurred in two successive days at Cerea and Alle due Castelli, owing to the extreme fatigue and a certain amount of disorder in the division Massena. As it was of importance not to leave Warmser outside of Mantua, and to prevent a fresh check, the troops were allowed to rest until noon; they waited till after dinner before they took up their arms, and the victory of San Giorgio was never for a moment doubtful.

To sum up, defensive battles are more in the sphere of mere professional routine; offensive battles, well prepared and well conducted, are affairs of genius. Such was also the true character of the wars of Frederick II., for the great defensive Seven Years' war had almost always an offensive character, and in that respect its campaigns bear much resemblance to many of Napoleon's campaigns, allowing for the differences of the times and of the state of the science of war.

When we read attentively the history of the actions of great generals, we may recognise the kind of troops they commanded by the mode in which they employed them. We can even recognise their actual character; for we must admit that those who excel in war of one kind have a special genius for that kind; the instinct we have derived from nature, if it be not our chief guide, at all events contributes powerfully to our faculties.

In all ages, great commanders have given their own particular physiognomy to their operations. Even those operations conducted by men most frequently compared to one another, present essential differences on close examination. The campaigns of Turenne and of the great Condé have no resemblance to one another; and the same is the case with regard to those of antiquity, *viz.*, those of Alexander, Caesar, and Fabius, of Hannibal and Scipio.

An able general, then, should, on entering on a campaign, make himself thoroughly master of the conditions in which he is placed by the nature and the number of his troops, the object he has to attain, the means at his disposal, and to regulate the best mode of employing them, even should that mode be not according to his own taste.

CHAPTER 7

On the Conduct of the Commander
After a Victory

Generals who win battles are more numerous than those who know how to turn the victory to profitable account. With many it would seem that the battle is the end, whereas it is only the means. This is especially noticeable in the wars of former times; but in our own days there is no lack of examples.

A commander of the ordinary stamp is occupied solely by. the losses he has himself experienced, and scarcely suspects those of the enemy; hence he displays fatal indecision and timidity, in place of that confidence that should enable him to dare anything.

In 1795, after the Battle of Loano, Scherer might, without any serious engagement, have invaded Italy. The same year Clairfait, after gaining his signal victory before Mainz, might have easily advanced to the walls of Strasburg, if he had marched without delay. In 1800, Moreau should have completed his successes at the opening of the campaign by rapid movements. The same year, in Italy, Brune, after crossing the Mincio and the Adige, might have utterly destroyed the Austrian Army which was in full retreat before him; the slightest energy would have sufficed, so much were circumstances in his favour.

Napoleon was the first in our times who drew from a victory all the consequences of which it was susceptible. After gaining a battle, he marched rapidly in pursuit of the enemy, in order to obtain easy successes, and to make him lose all the little confidence that still remained to him. With such a system, it was rarely necessary to fight a second battle in order to attain an important object.

No doubt, when a general acts in this way, he cannot attend very much to the wants of the army; hence the plan is attended with inconveniences, but these are insignificant in comparison with the advantages it ensures. Moreover, if the country traversed be fertile and thickly peopled, the sufferings of the soldiers will be slight, the march soon come to an end, and an important prize and immense resources fall into the victor's hands. Abundance and rest will afford to the commander the means of repairing his losses and augmenting his means besides. As long as Napoleon made war in Germany he acted in this manner, and found it answer very well. Vienna, which he occupied twice, furnished him with incalculable resources, and put in his hands a pledge of great value in the negotiations.

But there is a limit which cannot be overstepped with impunity. When this system of warfare was applied to Russia it was no longer a matter of ten or twelve quick marches through a country abounding in resources, and in the midst of a population mild in character and accustomed to respect and obey the laws; it was an offensive movement of nearly three months duration,[1] almost without a pause, in a poor country offering but few resources and among a population often hostile; and this movement had for its object not to pursue a vanquished army, but to reach in army that was falling back on its means, whilst we were consuming ours by the mere march, by the sufferings of all kinds to which our soldiers were exposed,[2] sufferings which soon occasioned a kind of disorganisation. Then Napoleon rushed into certain ruin.

If then it is true to lay it down as a great principle of war, that a commander should endeavour to profit by his successes, and should neglect nothing to render them complete by the rapidity of his movements in the pursuit of the vanquished army, it is also true that there are limits to this maxim, and that its application should be always subordinate to the special circumstances of the case.

But if a serious pursuit ought to be undertaken we should employ in it compact and powerful means, fitted to surmount all obstacles. If we do not, when we find ourselves obliged to stop, the courage of the enemy rises, and we behold the advantages we had a right to count upon slip away from us.

After the Battle of Wagram, Napoleon gave me, on the 8th of July,

1. The passage of the Niemen took place on the 23rd of Jane, the entrance into Moscow on the 4th of September, the movement therefore lasted 83 days.
2. The first corps on commencing the campaign was 85,000 men strong; when reviewed at Moscow it had only 15,000. The French cavalry on commencing the campaign was 50,000 strong; when reviewed at Moscow it numbered only 6,000.

the command of one of the advanced guards of the grand army. Massena followed the main force of the enemy's army in its retreat by the Hollabrun road. I was sent by the Nicolsburg road in pursuit of Prince Rosenberg, who was marching in that direction, and Marshal Davoust was ordered to join Massena. But the enemy retreated more slowly than I had anticipated, and two-thirds of his army was still on the hither side of the river, with almost all his material; one-third was in my front I took up a defensive position, in order to resist his efforts, and this position—which was not very far from Znaim—interfered with the retreating movement of the enemy at the passage of the bridge over the Taya.

In spite of repeated attempts he could not dislodge me; but still I was fully sensible of the fault I had committed in not requesting the assistance of Davoust, and of his mistake, in not coming spontaneously to my aid. The retreat of the enemy's army would have been cut off, and the main part of his forces obliged to retreat by very difficult by-ways, and to ascend the Taya—would probably have lost a great portion of his material, and been thrown into disorder. Had this success been obtained, the consequences would have been incalculable.

We ought not to demand assistance which we may consider superfluous, but we ought never to refuse it when offered. Some lucky opportunity may occur, which will give it an unexpected value.

CHAPTER 8

On Retreats

Great praise has always been accorded to retreats effected in the presence of a superior enemy, and with justice, for such operations are among the most delicate and risky that can be undertaken in war.

The principal difficulty is caused by the moral condition of the troops, which is apt to become much deteriorated in such circumstances. It is strange what a different impression is produced on the soldier according to whether he faces or turns his back to the enemy. In the former case he does not see what actually exists; in the latter his imagination magnifies the danger. Hence a commander should inspire his troops with pride and just confidence, and represent these sentiments as a powerful means of insuring their own safety.

The soldier should be made to understand that if he despises the enemy the enemy will respect him. In ordinary circumstances, when a commander ought to retire on the approach of the enemy, if there is no particular reason why he should prolong his stay in the locality he is about to quit, reason and prudence both require that he commence his movement before the enemy is in view. By leaving an interval of at least six miles, he makes his march more leisurely and easily. But it may so happen that it is necessary, above everything, to delay the advance of the enemy, to cause him to lose time by forcing him to make dispositions for an attack which shall be quite superfluous, because we retire at the moment the engagement seems about to commence. In such a case not only excellent troops are required but great precautions on the part of the commander are necessary. Safety depends on the disposition of the *échelons* and on the precision of the movements.

If the retiring corps is so disproportioned to the pursuing one, that there can be no idea of giving battle, it may still be able to sustain partial engagements without danger. For this purpose the commander of the retiring force should prepare his movements beforehand, in such a manner that there shall be no concision among his troops, and that they shall be able to march off easily and unencumbered. He should place with his rearguard a sufficient, but still not too strong, force of artillery, which should be well served, well harnessed and some of the guns of which should be of large calibre. This artillery, divided into two or three parts placed in *échelon*, will march with ease, and will prepare points of successive and temporary resistance. The enemy is thereby compelled to stop in order to make arrangements for attacking, and as soon as these arrangements are completed we move off again and disappear. The enemy then advances anew, but is kept at a distance by the fire of the artillery, which soon becomes stronger than his own; for the pursuing force elongates its columns, whilst the retiring force continually removes the field of battle to a greater distance and approaches its own reserves.

Hence there is a constant alternation of the relative strength of the troops that are in contact.

The 25th February, 1814, I executed a movement of this character with success. I was operating on the left bank of the Aube, and my corps consisted of about 6,000 men of all aims. The Prussian Army commanded by Marshal Blücher, 45,000 strong, crossed the River Plancy and marched against me. I took up a position on the heights of Vindé, behind Sezanne. The appearances were such as to suggest to the enemy's commander that I was resolved to fight He made complete arrangements for carrying the position, and placed thirty pieces of ordnance in battery. As soon as he had done this all my forces retired in an orderly, united and rapid manner, and the enemy pursued me; but during the march which lasted all day matters were conducted so that he was always kept at a distance, compelled to stop frequently in order to assemble his forces when he pressed me too closely. I arrived at Ferté-Graucher exchanging cannon shot all the way, and I took up a position behind the Morin. I had only lost those whom the enemy's balls had struck, and I did not leave behind a single living man, nor a single gun.

The day after the Battle of Brienne I was directed by Napoleon to retire on the Voire, and first to take a position at Perthe in order to engage the enemy's attention as long as possible, and so to make a diversion in favour of the main body of the troops retiring on the Aube by the Lesmont bridge. After having paraded my troops openly, and prepared the retreat so as to be able to make it with safety, I performed it without loss under the enemy's guns. I passed the defile of Rosnai without disorder, and as if we were on parade before the enemy's army, almost the whole of which was advancing upon me; he could not afterwards cross the Voire, although he attempted it several times.

If the retiring army is strong enough to fight the enemy, the dispositions it should make are similar. Its safety still consists in the manner in which the *échelons* are disposed, and the aim is always the application of the fundamental principle laid down above—to be more numerous than the enemy on the field at the moment of battle.

The best disposition to take in such a combination is the following:—To set out very early with the army, leaving a strong rear guard, which commences its march as late as possible without endangering itself; to take up a position in a defensible place at such a distance that the enemy cannot reach it until three hours before sunset However eager he may be to fight, he has not the time to make the preparatory dispositions, and, if he attempts to attack before he has made them, he should be beaten, for the encamped army has all its forces united, whereas he has only a portion of his.

It is thus that in 1812 the Army of Portugal, greatly inferior to the English Army, retreated in view of the latter from the banks of the Tormes in order to take up a position on the Douro, whence the enemy made no attempt to expel it.

In 1796, when General Moreau evacuated Bavaria in order to retire upon the Rhine, followed by the Austrian army, he put the above theory in practice; being pressed too closely, as he was marching with united forces, he stopped, gave battle, and obtained a victory.

But if a retreating army, or even a simple rear guard, should find an impregnable position on its route, which the enemy would be unable to carry unless, by turning it at a distance, it should always occupy it as long as it can remain without danger; should the enemy manoeuvre in order to cause it to be evacuated, his operations are thereby delayed, and the time gained is always advantageous to the army acting on the defensive. If the enemy, attacking precipitately in his impatience and eagerness, should throw himself against material obstacles, we should be able to gain an easy victory, sometimes inflicting great loss on the enemy, and possibly we may thereby effect a considerable change in the relative moral tone of the two armies.

This is what happened in Portugal on the 27th September, 1810. The English Army, inferior to the French, took part on the 26th ,on the hill of Busaco, a spur of the Sierra d'Accoba. The right of position which was impregnable barred the road, whilst the left, being attached to the superior mountains, was of easy access. Massena, whom the emperor had advised to take advantage of his superiority in order to force the enemy to accept battle, resolved to attack without delay, and unfortunately without having sufficiently reconnoitred the position occupied along all its front After prodigious efforts the corps of General Reignier succeeded in scaling the hill under the enemy's fire, but when it got on the plateau it found the English Army drawn up in order of battle, and was easily overpowered.

In a few minutes it lost the ground it had taken an hour to gain at a great cost of trouble and valour. Six thousand men were put *hors de combat*. The following morning, on seeing the French Army operating a movement on its right, the English Army disappeared. The result of this unfortunate battle was to change the moral tone of both armies; on one side it diminished that blind confidence so necessary to success, whilst it raised the spirit and the courage of the enemy. Had this not occurred we should probably have attempted an assault on the lines of Lisbon, and, had that been successful, the war in the Peninsula would have been ended.

CHAPTER 9

On Night Attacks and Surprises

It is impossible to lay down a theory respecting surprises. It ought to be impossible to execute a surprise during the day, and it would always be so if every officer and every soldier constantly did their duty with exactitude and intelligence: but sometimes this is far from being the case. When we succeed in surprising the enemy, it is a piece of good fortune we should know how to take advantage of, for it is one of the readiest and easiest ways of gaining a success.

Troops who are in the order of formation required by the circumstances—troops who know that they are going to fight, who are animated by a consciousness of their strength, by confidence—such troops attacking an enemy by surprise who is mot prepared to resist them, have such an advantage over him, that they have every right to count on victory.

Good troops, animated by an excellent spirit, commanded by an able general prompt in his resolutions, can alone escape a catastrophe, and that only sometimes, under such circumstances. But the truth is, that such troops and such a general would never conduct themselves so as to be placed in such a position.

It is otherwise with night attacks: here there may not be a surprise, properly speaking, but there is a sudden attack which could not have been foreseen, and there is ignorance respecting the real dispositions of the enemy; because at night we cannot perceive him until he is very close.

It is only when armies are very near one another, that I believe an enterprise of this nature to be possible; for were it necessary, before attacking, to traverse a great distance, there would be great danger that the various columns, when required to act, would fail to do so harmoniously.

It is then, I repeat, when two armies are very close to one another, that such an action could take place; only a moderate force should be employed, several points should be simultaneously attacked, and we should endeavour, before everything, to create disorder; should we succeed in doing so, we obtain the effects of a victory without having purchased it by great sacrifices, and we place ourselves in a position to profit by it if the state of things shall afterwards give us an opportunity of doing so.

This sort of thing should be chiefly attempted when we have opposed to us second-rate, ill-disciplined troops. If in the midst of the uncertainty of a real attack these troops commence to move, confusion will soon arise amongst them; sometimes, even, it will happen that the different columns do not know one another, and proceed to fire upon one another, to the great advantage of the assailants, who will then perform the part of the spectator. The commander of the attacking force employs only a portion of his troops, after giving them precise instructions determining the sphere in which they should operate, and making them acquainted with the position and direction of the other columns, so that it runs much less risk of falling into disastrous errors.

It has more than once happened that columns of one and the same army, during night operations, have taken one another for the enemy, and done much injury to each other.[1] If mere chance can produce such accidents, it may readily be imagined that it is possible to produce them designedly, and in that case the accidents are much more serious, because the presence of the enemy is a reality, and he may take part in the fray in a direct manner. It is sometimes good, therefore, when circumstances are very favourable, to attempt night attacks; to employ at first a limited number of troops who shall endeavour to render themselves masters of some important points, and hold themselves in readiness to overwhelm the enemy with all our forces as soon as day dawns, should we find it advantageous to do so.

The first example of an attack of this nature is the enterprise executed by the Austrian army on the Prussian Army at Hochkirchen in the night of the 13th and 14th October, 1758. The two armies were very close. Marshal Daun ably prepared his attack, which was very vigorously executed by General Laudon. The enterprise was favoured

---

1. Witness the accident that occurred to the Austrian Army at Karausebes, in 1789, under Joseph II. The different columns, taking one another for the enemy during the night, fired upon one another, and 6,000 men were put *hors de combat*.

by the blind confidence of Frederic the Great, who did not perceive the danger that menaced him. A sudden attack made in several columns rendered the Austrians masters of the large battery of the Prussian camp. Fighting was kept up till 10 o'clock in the morning, when the Prussian Army was forced to retreat, which it did in an orderly manner and without being pursued, after having lost almost all its artillery: to do this required good troops and the prestige of the name of the great captain who had been beaten.

But if the circumstances which allow of an enterprise of this character are rare and delicate, and if they require much consideration, there are others respecting which we should not hesitate, which are unattended with inconvenience in the case of failure, and which when successful give great results.

If beaten and retreating troops inconsiderately take up a position at night, without the protection of material obstacles, too close to the pursuing enemy, the circumstances are all in favour of the latter, who might very appropriately make a night attack with a few troops, but with vigour and intelligence.

On the evening of the Battle of Vauchamps I had the pleasure to make a very successful application of this principle.

The 14th February, 1814, after the disaster of the morning at Vauchamps, which cost the Prussian army 4,000 prisoners, the enemy retreated; my corps eagerly pursued him and I succeeded in surrounding his rearguard, composed of a Russian division, with my cavalry, increased by a reserve of mounted troops put at my disposal by Napoleon. This Russian infantry bravely resisted the charges made upon it and continued its march.

On its arrival at Etoges it was night, so under the cover of the wood it had traversed, it stopped and made arrangements for bivouacking. Napoleon had directed me to stop at Champ-Aubert and take up a position there, but I was well acquainted with the locality, having only quitted it the day before; knowing that the position of Etoges was as unfavourable for the enemy as it was favourable for us, and foreseeing that the following day I should be engaged in covering the movement which the emperor would make in order to get near the corps which were manoeuvring in the valley of the Seine, I thought I would hasten to attempt a *coup-de-main* upon this corps and not wait to occupy Etoges until it had taken its departure therefrom. I got together 800 infantry, I formed them in column on the high road, placing only fifty men on the right and left flank in the wood, at 100 paces, and marching along with them, I made the troops move in perfect silence, forbidding them to fire a single musket, and enjoining them to rush on the enemy as soon as they got sight of him.

It is three-quarters of a league from Champ-Aubert to Etoges; in half an hour we reached the enemy's advanced posts. The Russian troops occupied with their preparations for bivouacking, were dispersed, and only pickets and outposts were under arms. A bayonet charge put them all to flight; we rushed on the village; and in an instant, after having received scarcely 500 musket shots, all the infantry and artillery, numbering nearly 4,000 men, were in our power, together with their commander, Prince Ouroussow.

Thus, after a decided defeat and a hurried though orderly retreat, we should remove far enough from the enemy on the evening of the battle, to be safe from any attack by him; and after a decided success, we ought not to hesitate to make a night attack on the beaten enemy if he imprudently places himself within reach of his victor's blows.

I now come to speak of surprises, the design of which is to gain possession of a fortress. Many enterprises of this character have been performed; some have succeeded, others have failed, and though it may be difficult to discover precisely the circumstances which have influenced the results, still we may partly indicate them by finding out the conditions which should make them succeed.

When it is possible to execute such operations, we should not hesitate to attempt them. Their success sometimes changes the whole system and character of a war, and secures us greater advantages than the winning of a battle.

It is generally by means of establishing an understanding with the inhabitants that we are able to act. Sometimes they may be seduced by money bribes, but when religious or political passions are present, we may often meet with persons considered of honourable character who are willing to serve us. There are other enterprises where cunning, boldness, and courage are alone required for their successful execution, which have been suggested by the weakness or negligence of the garrison. Among the latter I should place the surprise of Prague by the French Army in 1741, which has rendered the name of Chevert celebrated; and the capture of Fort Mahon in 1766.

The fundamental principle for ensuring the success of a surprise, whether it be or be not favoured by the inhabitants of the town, is to get early possession of an entrance that leads, to the country. The number of troops that can be introduced furtively or by escalade is always very limited; it can never increase as rapidly as that of the troops who can rally to the defence, nor quickly enough to be formidable to a garrison on the defensive. Hence the chief aim should be to bring up as quickly as possible powerful reinforcements. Unless this condition be fulfilled, if the garrison and its commander do not become bewildered, such daring enterprises must always fail.

But we should always remember that even with everything in our favour, it is still possible to fail; if the surprised garrison is animated by an excellent spirit, if the soldiers are endowed with great energy, which prevents them calculating from the beginning either the disproportion of their forces to the imminent danger, whilst they think only of defending themselves and not of saving their lives. In that case every soldier will fight where he stands; the smallest bodies will take post everywhere; at the door of a house; at the comer of a street; behind a carriage; by doing so they unconsciously derange the enemy's combinations by delaying the advance of his first troops and thus a beginning is made to save the place. Every minute increases the chance of saving it; other troops, follow the example of the first, and soon the whole garrison is on foot, free from that powerful demoralisation that an unforeseen event always causes; they rally to one another; they act in combination, and come off victorious from a struggle in which it at first seemed that they would be worsted.

Under such circumstances, the first soldiers who find themselves in the enemy's presence, should have but one thought, that of the safety of all, and the glory which attends a great act of devotion.

This kind of feeling was never expressed with greater energy, never showed itself more gloriously than at the surprise of Cremona, on the 1st February, 1702. The character of the French soldier was never illustrated by a more glorious incident; it is unique in history, and shows what courage and valour can accomplish. Cremona was occupied by the head-quarters of the army and a garrison of 8,000 men; the great extent of the town, the negligent manner in which the service was performed, the feeling of security that prevailed, and the habitual neglect of military duties were remarked, and suggested to Prince Eugene of Savoy the idea of taking the place by surprise and capturing the garrison. The discovery of an ancient disused aqueduct favoured the enterprise; a traitorous curate, associated with some of the inhabitants, prepared it; 400 grenadiers in disguise were introduced and remained concealed in a church; other troops got in by the aqueduct

A walled-up gate was broken through during the night; 6,000

picked men, at the head of whom march Prince Eugene, the first general of the age, seemed to take possession of the town; finally, the enemy arrived on the square and occupied the principal communications before the garrison had got the alarm. At the cry, " the enemy is in the town," all awoke and ran to their arms; fighting began in all directions. Marshal de Villeroy was taken prisoner, all the generals except two were killed, wounded, or taken, and the direction of the defence was left entirely to the instinct of the soldiers; voices, which seemed providential, were heard indicating the movements and combinations requisite in order to save the town; and these troops, surprised in their beds, naked, without their officers, who endeavoured in vain to join them, fought desperately in the midst of this chaos for twelve hours, without food, drink or clothing, and it was mid winter; at length they drove out the enemy, after very nearly taking him prisoner.

And yet the only unforeseen events that occurred to this enemy, commanded by an illustrious captain, were encountering a battalion about to take its arms in order to go to drill, and the delay of a reinforcement of 4,000 men, on which it reckoned, and whose business it should have been to prevent the flight and escape of the garrison. A more splendid feat of arms was never accomplished! If, in such extraordinary and discouraging circumstances, a garrison was able by its energy to secure its safety, we may fancy what ought to happen when a garrison does not lose heart at the first view of danger, but offers resistance to a weak detachment that has surprised an entrance; when the disproportion of numbers between the attacking and defending parties is so great, one hour's resistance will decide the event, for it does away with the effects of the unexpected, which are so powerful, and brings things into the domain of reality, which, whatever it may be, is a thousand times less formidable than that of imagination.

In recent times an event, analogous to that I have just spoken of, occurred to the credit of our troops; it is less generally known, but it may be useful to recall it to mind and to transmit the circumstances to posterity.

In 1814, when the events of the war had taken us to a distance from the banks of the Rhine, Holland was evacuated, and immediately became hostile to France. Some English troops under the command of General Graham soon disembarked there in order to sustain public spirit and to impart consistency to the revolution that was going on.

General Molitor, on quitting Holland, left garrisons in the most important strongholds; but the state of our armies at that time did not allow of a large force being employed in this service, and probably they were only composed of *depôt* battalions. The garrison of Berg-op-Zoom, in consideration of its importance and extent, accumulated to 4,000 men. Those conscripts who did not belong to France proper, having deserted, its numbers were reduced to 3,000, and it was with this weak force that the brilliant feat of arms, I am about to relate, was performed—a feat that redounds as much to the glory of this handful of heroes as to that of General Bizanet who commanded them.

The measures taken by the latter before the event were of the wisest and most far-sighted character, and those that followed them, when the moment of action arrived, were still more energetic. Here it was not as at Cremona, where deliverance from danger was due solely to the dogged courage of the troops. At Berg-op-Zoom the soldiers were also extremely brave, resolute and energetic, but it was chiefly by their submission to the rules of discipline, and by their docile obedience to the voice of their chief, that they triumphed over the enemy.

The garrison being insufficient General Bizanet had concentrated all his troops in the town and evacuated the outworks in which his small troop would have been lost. He made up for the inconveniences, as regards surveillance resulting from this measure, by very frequent patrols. He doubled the interior posts, and established numerous night pickets always prepared to take up arms.

General Graham, who commanded the English in Holland, finding himself in the neighbourhood of Berg-op-Zoom, and being informed of the small number of its defenders, imagined he could capture it by a *coup-de-main*. He also relied on the assistance of the inhabitants, and had an understanding with some of them inside. He took 4,800 men for his enterprise, and he selected the night between the 8th and 9th of March—the anniversary of the Prince of Orange's birth—to put it into execution.

The assailant divided his force into four columns for four simultaneous attacks. The two first were to scale the rampart; one betwixt the Antwerp gate and the harbour, the other between the Antwerp and Breda gates; a third was to show itself before the Strasburg gate and make a false attack there; finally, the fourth was to enter the town by the harbour, availing itself of the low tide.

At 10 p.m., the third column surprised the advanced post of the Strenberg Gate, but it was stopped short by the fire of troops placed in a stockade for the purpose of defending the bridge at night. The garrison flew to its arms.

At the same instant the fourth column entered by the harbour without being perceived by the guard-boat, and penetrated into the town. But troops sent against it divided it; one part was stopped and captured, whilst the other part penetrated to the rampart, where it was followed.

The second column had succeeded in scaling the wall, and marched upon the Antwerp gate, in order to throw it open to General Graham, who was waiting on the glacis with the remainder of his troops and his cavalry. But a strong picket, sent hurriedly by General Bizanet as a reinforcement to the Antwerp gate, prevented the English from gaining possession of it, whilst the first column failed in its attempt to scale the rampart, and was driven back with great loss. Thus there was fighting going on in different directions all night.

As soon as day began to dawn, General Bizanet attacked with the rest of his troops, hurled the enemy towards the gate leading towards the sea, and thus got them into a corner. Not being able to escape, and crushed by the grape of the outworks, the English columns were forced to lay down their arms, with the loss of 1,200 dead, 600 wounded, among them two general officers, and 2,177 prisoners, among whom were one general and four colonels, 4,000 muskets, four standards, a large quantity of munition, &c.

General Graham begged for an armistice for three days in order to bury his dead, remove his wounded, and receive his prisoners on parole. Eulogy for an action of this sort would be superfluous.

Thus it will be seen that at all periods French valour has maintained its glorious reputation; our manners attach an extraordinary éclat to military glory, and this appreciation of that which demands the sacrifice of life, a sacrifice which public applause alone can worthily recompense, has greatly contributed to develop in France the virtues of self-sacrifice, the safeguard of the preservation and of the might of nations. The army will not change as long as our manners remain what they are. May Heaven grant that no change may take place in this respect, and that those cold, reasoning minds, who only see a warranty for social happiness in national prosperity, and whose disastrous aberrations prove their complete ignorance of the human heart, never exercise any power or obtain any credit in the councils of our country that would be fatal to its well-being!

I cannot recall to mind any instances of strongholds defended by French troops being surprised; but such things have frequently happened among foreign nations. I shall relate two which happened to the Prussians during the Seven Years' War, that of Galatz in 1760, and that of Schweidnitz in 1761.

General Laudon had some time previously established an understanding with several officers among the garrison in the fortress of Galatz, by means of monks residing in the town. No sooner had the Austrians arrived before the stronghold than they opened their trenches, and being informed of the moment when the officers devoted to them were on guard in the advanced fort, called the Crane, which was hollowed out of the rock and seemed to be impregnable, they directed a sudden assault against it; the besieged fled, and the Austrians, who eagerly followed them, entered the fortress *pêle-mêle* with them. Troops which were at hand followed the first assailants, and the Austrians carried the place without having met with the slightest resistance.

The Schweidnitz affair was as follows:—Five hundred prisoners of war were there, and among them an Italian major, of the name of Boca, an officer of irregulars; this officer ingratiated himself with the commandant, and was allowed to walk freely about the fortress. He soon made himself acquainted with the distribution of the posts and the details of the service. He carried on intrigues in the town, and busied himself with corrupting those who might be of use to him. Moved by his reports, General Laudon conceived the project of surprising the place, and this he carried into execution on the night betwixt the 30th September and the 1st October. He divided twenty battalions into four attacking bodies.

The *commandant* of Schweidnitz was at a ball, but something occurred to alarm him and he had the garrison under arms, but he omitted to send anyone outside in order to ascertain if the enemy were near, so that the Austrians got right up to the palisades without being discovered; they surprised the Stricgauet Gate; in the confusion the prisoners of war got possession of the interior gate, and in less than an hour the town was taken and the garrison made prisoners.

I shall say a few words more relative to two more surprises that were attempted in modern times, but which did not succeed, solely owing to the manner in which they were conducted.

When the French Army was about the make the siege of Mantua, in 1796, it was thought possible and advantageous, the very first night, to carry the work by surprise; this work, which had no revetment, covered a long curtain of the body of the place only flanked by two large towers; it then made and continued, until we constructed the

Fort Pictoli, to make the best defence of Mantua on that side. The garrison was said to be weak and exhausted with sickness. Three hundred soldiers were made to assume the uniform of one of the regiments in the fortress, and put under the order of an Italian officer who had deserted from the Austrians and was in our service. He was to pretend to be defending the island on which the fort is situated, to make believe that he was closely pressed by the French troops, to rush upon the barrier of the covered way as though seeking an asylum there, to get it open to him, to take possession of it, and thus secure an entrance to the fort.

But this officer was very afraid of falling into the hands of the Austrians and being hung by them, so he performed his part very mildly, whilst Murat, who commanded the troops that were to support him, acted slowly and circumspectly. This slowness betrayed the whole trick to the garrison: such a ruse could only succeed by extraordinary activity and quickness.

The other was the enterprise made in 1800 on the Fort of Bard. The garrison numbered scarcely 150 men. The assault which was made would certainly have succeeded had it been conducted with discernment. Colonel Dufour —a brave soldier, but entirely destitute of intelligence and incapable of reflection—being charged with the command of the column that was to carry the door, in place of approaching silently, and noiselessly placing his ladder against the wall—which ought to have been scaled in one instant—took upon himself—like a blockhead as he was—to have the charge beaten before leaving the village where he lay. The garrison, warned in time, was prepared for the defence. Dufour got a ball through his chest, and the attack was repulsed with considerable loss. This check rendered necessary the bold and unexampled enterprise of having the artillery drawn by the men under the fort at night, and in spite of the enemy's fire, and so passing the defile.[2]

---

2. I am entitled to claim for myself the merit of the conception and execution of this audacious enterprise, all the details of which I directed in person. The First Consul had nothing to do with it, except that he gave me leave to attempt it; but justice demands that I should give some of the credit to the chief of my staff, then Lieutenant-Colonel De Sénarmont, an officer of great skill and courage, who afterwards became Lieutenant-General, and was killed before Cadiz. He contributed greatly to the success of the scheme, by the assistance he gave me. This officer bore a name renowned in connection with the artillery, his father having been an illustrious officer of that arm.

CHAPTER 10

On the Defence of Fortresses

The first element of resistance in a stronghold is a good *commandant*; add to this first indispensable condition a garrison of sufficient strength, and large stores of all sorts, provisions, munitions, &c., and you will be able to obtain the most extraordinary results.

Fortifications may be more or less perfect, but this perfection, however desirable, is but a trifle compared with the effects produced by the courage and resolution of the man who presides over the defence. The governor of a fortress is its soul—it lives in and by him. If the garrison is bad at the commencement of a siege it will soon become good under a good commandant; he will be able to awaken in it sentiments of honour, patriotism, and glory, which sometimes lie dormant in the hearts of soldiers.

It is a fine thing to gain battles; the glory which redounds to the chief dazzles; success excites enthusiasm and admiration; but it is a still finer, or at least more meritorious thing to defend a fortress beyond a certain time.

The glory of a battle won, how great soever it may be for the commander, is always shared by others—that of the governor of a fortress belongs to himself almost entirely. This glory is his own work—it is the fruit, not of a single action performed under certain circumstances, but of a long and uninterrupted series of persevering efforts constantly renewed, with an ever-present sense of their uselessness should timely assistance not arrive; and the efforts of each day are not rewarded by the prospect of the pleasures of a victory; on the contrary, they are always associated with the painful feeling of relative weakness, and have not for their aim to triumph over the enemy, but only to defer his success without changing the results.

Every man of spirit can always display courage and energy during twenty-four hours. In success every man seems to be a hero; but how rare it is to find the same courage, the same tenacity, the same ardour under defeat; it is only the truly brave that can do this, and they are not so very numerous.

But the governor of a besieged fortress is in still more difficult circumstances; not only does he require to preserve the moral courage Providence so rarely endows men with, but his courage should increase as the circumstances become more difficult, when it naturally would tend to decrease, for he must display enough of it to act upon the garrison as a counterpoise to the sufferings and misery they have to endure.

The governor alone seems interested in maintaining the defence, because he almost alone reaps the glory of it, whilst those under his command get nothing but the sufferings. So when a governor is inclined to surrender, he will always find around him persons to approve of his doing so, and officers disposed to remove all his scruples and doubts; and when a council is assembled to vote whether the time has come to capitulate, this question is always decided in the affirmative; and it even sometimes happens that those who protest against the surrender would not give expression to their opinion if their vote could change the majority the other way.

There is, then, nothing more admirable than the defence of a fortress carried to the utmost possible limits, but at the same time nothing is rarer. Justice, therefore, demands that the names of those who have earned glory of this sort should be immortalised.

The finest defence known in the history of modern wars is that of Grave, on the Meuse, by M. de Chamilly, in 1675—nothing is comparable to it. This town had received the *depôts* of the army at the time of the invasion of Holland by Louis XIV., and it contained immense stores. It was but of moderate extent; it had a garrison of 6,000 men; it defended itself during five months of open trenches; resisted all the efforts of the Prince of Orange, who lost before it 30,000 men; and Chamilly only surrendered on an order signed by the king, and carried off with him all the pieces of ordnance stamped with the arms of France.[1]

---

1. My ambition has always been to be entrusted with the defence of a large fortress, believing, as I do, that such a task would not be beyond my powers. Had I been placed in this position I should have caused to be reprinted the *Journal of the Siege of Grave*, so that every officer, non-commissioned officer, and private might have had a copy. If regiments should ever have libraries, it would be useful to have in them this work, which is most instructing to every soldier.

After this admirable defence we should next reckon that of Lille and its citadel in 1708. Marshal de Boufflers, who was in command, acquired immortal glory there.

In our time sieges have been rare; we should not, however, omit to mention the defence of St Sebastian, commanded by General Rey—a long and obstinate defence, which post the English a great number of men.

The defence of the Fort of Burgos, under the orders of General Dubreton, who was attacked by less powerful forces, was not inglorious, neither was that of Wittemberg, on the Elbe, by General La Poype.

But for the few extraordinary resistances which deserve our admiration how many defences have there not been that were of a very poor character which have been judged with unmerited leniency?—how many culpable surrenders perpetrated with impunity?

The retention of a stronghold is so important and vital an affair—it sometimes exercises such a powerful influence on the safety of an army and of a whole country—that its surrender should always be made the subject of a legal investigation, to elicit the circumstances that have accompanied the defence and induced the capitulation. Therefore, the governor should either be punished or rewarded and loaded with praise. I cannot admit of any middle course between these two.

The navy regulations require that any captain who loses his ship, in whatever way that should have happened, should be put upon his trial. If he have done his duty he is acquitted and dismissed with honour.

We can understand such indulgence and leniency in the execution of the laws, because, on an element so mobile as the sea, circumstances of an overwhelming force may occur powerful enough to gain the mastery over science, vigilance, and courage; but on land nothing is variable. When the capitulation is not caused by a want of food there can be no legitimate excuse for it—we have no choice but to blame or to praise. Military orders should be rigorously executed; and when a governor surrenders before a practicable breach has been made in the defences, and before having sustained at least one assault, he has been guilty of a crime, and he ought to be punished.

I shall not enter into the technical details of the attack and defence of fortresses; these matters have been treated exhaustively in special treatises; I shall content myself with making some reflections on the general directions to be followed in the defence.

In the case of large fortified towns, it is too much the habit to make sorties to a distance before the commencement of the siege, and thus to waste a portion of the means, the forces and the confidence that are so useful and so important to save for the time when courage and vigour are most necessary. In moving to a distance from the fortifications, we lose their support and deprive ourselves of an auxiliary which establishes a sort of equilibrium between the troops of the garrison and those of the attacking army. I should advise, therefore, that in no case, unless there is a probability of being able to raise the siege, should a sortie made with a large part of the garrison go so far as to be deprived of the efficacious support of the guns of the fortress.

But if such sorties should be prohibited, those intended to destroy works just commenced cannot be too frequent, the principal aim being to retard the enemy's advance and to gain time. These objects will be obtained by causing him frequent alarms, by fighting many sharp but short engagements, forcing him to recommence over and over again the same works. As the enemy approaches the fortress and the siege advances, sorties made with fewer men, as the battlefield becomes ever more limited, ought to be more frequent. Finally, it is just at the time when the great proximity of the enemy so often suggests to governors the notion of capitulating, that real defence ought to commence: indeed it would seem that it ought never to terminate, if new obstacles be prepared every day, if suitable interior defensive works be constructed, and if such dispositions be made that the besieged shall never be completely deprived of the fire of their guns, but shall always succeed in preserving some pieces of ordnance well covered for the defence of the breach. This precaution which should be particularly attended to might of itself determine the fate of the fortress for many days and add much to the glory of the defence.

I shall conclude this chapter by an observation that concerns the governors of besieged fortresses. They should always be particularly careful to guard against surprises, for the more improbable an event is the more effect does it produce when it takes place. A brave garrison defends a breach, and for a long time the enemy cannot overcome their resistance; but if at the moment when attention is all directed to the defence of an open point, the defenders become aware that the enemy has penetrated by scaling ladders into the stronghold at another point, then they become distracted in their minds, the defence of the breach is abandoned and the fortress is taken.

A strict watch over every point should, therefore, always be maintained, and we should be particularly careful to keep an eye on those which seem least attackable, for these are just the points the enemy will select by preference, because as such points seem to be self-defended no one will trouble himself about them.

In 1741, Prague was the object of very noisy nocturnal demonstrations by the French army on two points, and these demonstrations attracted the whole attention of the garrison, but other troops crept silently to a point of the rampart of the new town, at a great distance from the others; they took with them only a single ladder,—they mounted the wall, and finding no one there, they opened a neighbouring gate, and the town, together with its garrison, was taken with scarcely any fighting.

In our days, in 1812, at Rodrigo, the garrison bravely defended a practicable breach made in the body of the place, and repulsed the enemy; but 50 English soldiers, with ladders, escaladed the castle—a dominant point—the scarp of which has a revetment, and from a great height raised the alarm, produced disorder, and became master of the town.

So also at Badajoz, which was besieged the same year; the garrison was a good one, commanded by General Philippon, a distinguished officer, who only the year previously had sustained a glorious siege. Entrenched on the breach, he there repulsed the assaults of the enemy; but the castle, the walls of which were 80 feet high, was escaladed by 50 men; alarm and disorder arose, and the town was taken.

Under no pretext should vigilance be relaxed, but there should also be at hand, even in those places apparently safest from an attack, some means of offering resistance, especially when the siege has commenced, and when the enemy might naturally suppose that all the means of defence are concentrated at the points where his attacks are directed.[2]

---

2. Among remarkable defences I have not alluded to that of Saragossa, by the Spaniards, because it belongs to another order of events. A large population, refugees from the provinces, with immense stores—a population rendered fanatical by religion and patriotism—whose numbers were always more than double those of the besieging force, and whose daily losses were inappreciable, occupying those enormous and indestructible convents, which are quite fortresses, would naturally long arrest our efforts. But it is scarcely likely that such circumstances will happen again. This defence cannot teach any lesson that could be of utility in regular warfare. As to the siege of Genoa, it was no doubt a grand operation of war, but it was the defence of an entrenched camp and not of a fortress properly so called.

CHAPTER 1

On the Habits of Soldiers, and the Way to Form Them, On the Armies of the Past and Those of the Present

Three things are necessary to give value to troops: love of order, habits of obedience, confidence in themselves and in others. Such, in a moral point of view, are the fundamental bases of an army. Without these bases an assemblage of men has no consistence, justifies no hopes, satisfies no wants.

Nothing, therefore, should be neglected in order to develop these three elements in the mind and in the heart of the soldier, and to infuse into his moral nature those habits which I will call military virtues.

Discipline—in other words, submission to the law and the will of the legal chief—should be kept up without any relaxation; and every one, whatever place he occupies in the hierarchy, should constantly bear in mind that he only commands his subordinates in virtue of the obedience he owes his superiors.

Discipline, always severe for a grave fault should admit of modifications in its application.

In countries where elevation of sentiment, delicacy of manner, and dignity of character do not admit of corporal punishments, it is of importance to bring opinion to bear on punishments as much as possible.

The French Army in particular has always given an intelligent chief numerous opportunities of employing this agent. Praise and blame appropriately distributed—the talent of exciting a useful and noble emulation, have often sufficed for all needs. Punishments and rewards, based upon opinion, are in so far admirable, that they are susceptible of infinite shades, and act powerfully on generous minds.

No punishment, whatever it may be, unless for an act of flagrant cowardice, should be inflicted with expressions of contempt. Everything that degrades and disgraces the soldier diminishes the value of the man, just as everything that elevates him in his own eyes adds to his faculties. There are a thousand ways of varying the expression of those sentiments; an able chief selects with discernment the means that are best adapted to the kind of men he has to deal with, and to the circumstances in which he is placed.

In some armies severity towards derelictions that in the eye of reason appear to be trivial is carried to excess. Though I am not prepared to condemn this system, I cannot approve of the importance attached to it by its supporters. A severe punishment awarded for something out of order in the accoutrements, or for some momentary failure of immobility when under arms, is not reasonable; but moderate punishment for such faults has its uses in a moral point of view. The spirit of order and respect for the law are everywhere felt; and they must be upheld as a part of the education, and of the habits of life. A soldier whose coat is dirty would no doubt fight as well as one whose uniform is in good order, but one who is careless in respect to his daily duties will probably be inattentive to the commands of his superior officer.

The existence of an army is such a wonderful, such an artificial thing, that we cannot, without danger, neglect anything that contributes to impart to it habits of order and submission. But the chief should be able to perceive clearly the real end, without exaggerating the importance of the means.

The officers and chiefs should do their utmost to inspire their soldiers with confidence; unless this bond unites them, nothing can be safely reckoned on. In times of peace, the regular power is respected and obeyed readily; but in the midst of the perturbation danger gives rise to, everything becomes complicated, and the smallest natural obstacle may become insurmountable. Then it is that confidence in one's self and in others, that powerful internal voice, gives extraordinary energy that leads to success.

The chief should therefore see to the well-being of the soldier; he should know how, on important occasions to share his sufferings and privations, to watch over the maintenance of order and discipline, to punish when necessary, and to seize with avidity on the opportunity of awarding recompenses; but these recompenses should be merited, for confidence in the justice of a chief is the foundation of his credit, and of the feeling of his men towards him. The instinct of men is clever at discovering when their chief is worthy of them. When this is so his severity does not alarm or hurt, for it implies strength, and strength, when it is the sincere interpreter of the laws, ensures the efficacious protection of rights. Even those who come under its action feel at the bottom of their hearts how useful and worthy of respect it is.

As the maintenance of order ought to be a constant care for the chiefs of all degrees, so love of the soldier should be deeply graven on their hearts. I repeat, how can we avoid loving this deserving class of men whose condition is, on the whole, so hard; who are so habituated to privations; whose lives are made up of so many sacrifices; who pass their best years in the midst of painful labour—of incessantly recurring dangers; and who attach themselves so sincerely to their chief when he loves them! The soldier is good by nature. If he is disqualified for the highest ranks of society by his wants of enlightenment, he is worthy of them by the sentiments that animate him. His habit of obedience to law renders him more moral A life fraught with dangers develops the noble instincts of the heart, and accustoms him to self-sacrifice—a sentiment inspired by Heaven itself. On his return home the soldier is almost always an example to the social circle amid which he lives. I have seen him, in the midst of the horrors and atrocities that war sometimes engenders, distinguish himself by acts of holy piety and of Christian charity.[1] May shame and misfortune be the lot of all who do not honour him, or who do not make every effort to improve and to sweeten his existence!

Another duty which ought never to be neglected is to keep the troops always actively employed. Activity should be to them a second nature. Like almost all men they are inclined to be lazy. It is doing them a great service to prevent their becoming so. Repose and idleness diminish strength and valour. Health, energy and moral courage, usually result from a life hardened by fatigue and accustomed to exercise.

1. I could mention many examples of this kind, but I shall content myself by recalling one only. During the Egyptian campaign, a village revolted; and a military execution was necessary, by way of example. The village was burned, and almost all the inhabitants were put to the sword. A soldier, who no doubt had had his share of cruelty, was melted at the sight of an infant that stretched his arms towards him. He put it on his knapsack, took a goat to nurse it, carried the child for eight days, and dragged the goat along with him, until he met with an Arab woman, who was willing to adopt the child.

Drilling is the first element of this activity which I insist on, but it is not the only one. The first thing required by the soldier is the most thorough instruction; when he has acquired that, to occupy him with the details he is familiar with, which teach him nothing further, is an infallible way to render his profession hateful to him:

Grand reviews that make a fine show are the only things he never tires of; but we may also create new interests for him by exciting emulation in games of various kinds. We may also employ him on important public works, and, as a reward, connect the history of a regiment with the works they have executed by giving them its name. In this way we may economically carry out some grand designs, whilst at the same time we develop in our troops ideas of immortal glory and greatness, which cannot be too much encouraged in the minds of soldiers.

Throughout my military career I never let slip an opportunity of applying this principle, and I have always had reason to be satisfied with the result, with regard both to the immediate object in view, and to the effect on the spirit of the troops. But I took care never to go beyond certain limits, and never to compromise in any way the military spirit, whose preservation and development should always be the aim of all the efforts of commanders. Egypt, Holland, and Dalmatia, still show monuments of our past greatness, and of our former habits. In the last mentioned country 80 leagues of beautiful roads, made in the wildest localities, in the midst of the greatest natural difficulties, remain to the inhabitants an honoured remembrance of our presence which will never pass away. Inscriptions cut in the rocks doubtless still inform the traveller that these works were performed by such and such regiments, under such and such colonels. And when these brave soldiers—whose memory is so dear to me—laid aside their tools to resume their arms, what renown did they not acquire on the battlefield! What strength, what energy, did they not display during the longest marches, amid the greatest fatigues!

Among the complementary means of forming troops, I consider one of the chief to be the establishment of large camps of instruction. In times of peace, they alone can give to troops the habits and the instruction they require. The military spirit is only developed in the midst of the dangers of war and the assemblages of troops which resemble war. Camp life, the movement that accompanies it, the mixture of all arms, this peculiar mode of life so widely different from civil society, and which is the element of success and glory, can only be called into being by assemblages of some duration and in the midst of prosperity. I do not refer to those momentary assemblages which we see taking place in different countries, the object of which is rather to make a display than to give instruction and develop the faculties, but of those camps of my youth, whence issued the first and best army that has been seen in modern times, and which if it may be equalled will certainly never be surpassed: I refer to the army which was encamped for two years on the coasts of the Channel and the North Sea, and which fought at Ulm and Austerlitz.

Fortified by this example and convinced by my reflections, I should like to see permanent establishments formed in provinces which have but a wretched kind of cultivation, such as Champagne; and durable barracks constructed to hold 30,000 men. The same troops would occupy them for at least three months. Three such establishments would suffice to preserve in the French Army the military spirit and the instruction which would render it constantly ready for war. But at the present moment we have a still larger exercising field, Algiers, which if its advantages are dearly purchased, gives a rich dower to the army in respect to what I have just been considering.

I cannot conclude this chapter without entering into some details relative to the manner in which the regular armies were formed in Europe. It is curious to notice in what respects the armies of former times differed as to their compositions from the armies of the present day: the consequences to be drawn from this comparison will strike anyone who considers it attentively.

After the invasion of the barbarians and the destruction of the Roman power, all special military organisation disappeared in Europe. For many ages, the only basis the armies had was the feudal constitution. When experience showed the weakness of these temporary assemblages of men called together in haste and without rule, and whom the caprice of the lords or the exigencies of their wants would suddenly disperse, rendering the execution of any operation demanding calculation impossible, it was sought to create means of regular and permanent military power.

The sovereigns nominally invested with the right were actually without any real power over their vassals. In order to emancipate themselves from this state of dependence when their finances allowed them, they wanted to have troops of their own, and thus arose the companies of "*ordonnance.*"

But regular revenues were required in order to maintain troops constantly under arms; and, on the other hand, regular revenues are not obtainable without order and a certain amount of administrative organisation: the creation of armies was thus the cause and the means of a commencement of civilisation.

However, as the feudal system put the populations into the hands of the lords, the latter were far from favourable to the establishment of troops destined to overthrow their own power; the sovereigns having only their private domains to dispose of, which were of very limited extent, were reduced to voluntary enlistments for the sake of pay.

The disorders that existed throughout Europe—the constant wars that were being waged; the large number of petty sovereigns rendered the populations miserable, and held out the profession of soldier as a livelihood. The manners of the times, moreover, allowed any one to cherish the hopes of boundless ambition.

A warrior could aspire to everything; and the only element in his schemes was his own personal ambition. It was very different in those days to what it is now, when the sole thoughts of the soldier are to fulfil his duly towards his sovereign; to defend his native land, and to acquire glory—that reward of opinion so highly valued in our times. Private or officer, every one sought to acquire wealth; and often raised his aspirations to the throne itself. Visconti, Sforza, Escales, Ecelini, and many others, had no other origin; and before them kingdoms had been the prey of some Norman adventurers. The sovereigns, in order to facilitate the execution of their projects, were always forced to employ as their agents soldiers of repute, who, addicted to the profession of arms from their youth, were acquainted with many men able to assist them—with whom they formed alliances for their mutual benefit.

Each in his separate sphere had his own dependents, and regiments were provided on commission and by competition.

Ferdinand II. summoned Wallenstein, and requested him to raise an army. The conditions were discussed and the treaty signed. Wallenstein called together officers who enjoyed his confidence, and asked them to provide regiments, giving them a share in his emoluments. These latter summoned the captains, who took upon themselves to raise companies and to find soldiers, and thus the army was formed. The whole transaction resembled what happens in our own days when a sovereign negotiates a loan with a rich banker. The latter distributes the greater portion of the loan among his correspondents, associating them with the profits he calculates on making, while these last seek the money they require in the pockets of private individuals.

It is easy to see that an organisation of this sort gave the colonel who raised the regiment a sort of proprietary interest in it.

Hence the name they received, and which they still preserve in Austria; where, though they have become the regiments of the sovereign, as in every other country, they still retain to some degree their primitive physiognomy and a peculiar constitution and privileges. Moreover, the system followed there, which has put the institutions in harmony with the interests of the State, and with the manners of modern times, offers at once a noble and splendid reward to those generals whose life has been rendered illustrious by glorious services, and guarantees to the sovereign for the good selection of the officers and the excellent spirit of the troops.

I may here allude to the immense difference between the composition of armies in former times and now-a-days. The armies of our days are raised by a compulsory recruitment. This is the case in all European states with the exception of England, where peculiar circumstances explain the maintenance of a system which exists in no other country. modern armies are too numerous to admit of their being raised solely by voluntary recruiting; moreover, the class of men for whom military service is a resource necessary for their existence is not sufficiently numerous—public order, which, fortunately, everywhere prevails, diminishes immensely the number of that class.

Finally, the chances of success in the career of arms are too small to attract men of birth to choose it for their profession. Other channels are open by development of trade and commerce to all who are gifted with zeal and intelligence, and there they may make their fortunes without danger. Compulsory recruiting is, therefore, the only way to satisfy the requirements of the state for its defence; hence the blood-tax has everywhere become one of the public imposts.

The spirit of armies has been greatly modified by this change; but it is far from being a loser thereby, in spite of appearances. Voluntary recruiting, accompanied by a terrible discipline, has sometimes furnished good troops, as in England; but can any comparison in respect of spirit and morality be made between an army composed of respectable young men, brought up in a spirit of order and of obedience to the laws, and one which—though it may, perhaps, contain some individuals animated by the love of war and glory—is mainly composed of vagabonds, whose evil habits have excluded them from all decent and laborious modes of obtaining a livelihood?

How much securer is the public interest when it is confided to those who regard military service as a noble and important duty? The young man of peaceful habits, on whom the lot has fallen, may quit his family with regret—nay, with pregnant sorrow—but the warlike spirit so natural to man, and especially to the Frenchman, soon descends upon him; he then nourishes himself with noble thoughts, he grows greater in his own eyes, he is faithful, devoted, and he looks for the reward of his sacrifices, his toils and his dangers, to the good opinion of his chief and comrades. Such is the European soldier of the present day—for the , system is the same everywhere.

It now remains for us to consider which is the preferable of the two prevailing systems: to place the recruits from the same countries in regiments by themselves, or to distribute them among different corps. The first plan is adopted in Austria, Prussia, and Germany; the second in France and Russia. Each has its advantages and its inconveniences, but I prefer the first system.

To commence with the inconveniences. This system gives to the soldiers a local and provincial spirit, which after the numerous revolutions we have experienced would not be without danger in certain circumstances that may readily be imagined; perhaps also in time of peace it lessens the military spirit and tends to make an assemblage of peasants rather than of soldiers; but these are inconveniences easily remedied by increasing the frequency of assemblages of regiments and prolonging the duration of the camps of instruction.

As to the advantages, they are great and incontestable. As regards the administration, recruiting is easier; the officers of the corps have the means of watching over the men when on leave, and the transition from a peace to a war footing is immensely simplified. In a moral point of view the feeling of honour—and this is a great thing—is heightened, and this feeling renders all the men participators in the glory of their regiment, while it at the same time makes them anxious to defend the reputation of the province where they were born. It is an additional spur, a fresh encouragement.

Again; a distinguished soldier is rewarded for good conduct by the esteem of his corps, but the system pursued in France deprives him of this advantage when he leaves the service. On his return home no one knows him: he loses the worthiest prize of his life—the renown he has acquired.

On the other hand, his renown would follow him to his home, did he there meet with the companions of his youth; he would remain until death surrounded by the halo of glory he had deservedly acquired.[3]

---

3. This question occupied the attention of the Council of War in 1823. General D'Ambrugeac, one of the most distinguished officers of the army, the reporter of the Infantry Committee, brought forward a mixed system, which, while creating an excellent reserve, resolved the question most satisfactorily. An adverse fate decreed that almost all the labours of this Council, where military questions were debated and deliberated on carefully, came to nought.

CHAPTER 2

On the Military Spirit and the Difficulties of the Command

The assemblage of 100,000 men in one place, far from their families, their property and their interests; their docility, their obedience, their mobility and their sustenance; finally, the spirit that animates them, and, at a signal given by one man, leads them to rush with pleasure into imminent danger, where many of them meet with their death—surely this is one of the most extraordinary spectacles that social man can show; it is a phenomenon whose cause and principle are among the mysteries of the human heart.

It belongs to our nature to love emotions and to seek for them. The idea of danger pleases us, though at the crisis there are few men who are not disconcerted by it. But we require to compare ourselves with others; emulation is natural to us; everyone loves to believe and to see himself superior to his fellows. Such is the exciting cause in virtue of which the instinct of self preservation gives place to the noble displays of courage.

The sphere of activity in which self love acts, depends on the situation of individuals. Everyone desires to be seen and admired. The man placed in a crowd, has hid horizon limited by what immediately surrounds him; in a more elevated position this horizon is enlarged; when at the highest point, the whole world sees him.

This feeling, so honourable to a man, is the main spring of the most generous actions. It is the spur of action to the simple soldier as well as to the general. Then in all ranks the profession of arms is noble, because for all, it consists of sacrifices, and has its chiefest reward in popular esteem and glory. To speak contemptuously of those who make up the rank and file of the army, is a sort of blasphemy; even to speak of them with indifference is to misunderstand the conditions of our nature.

The elevated sentiment I have just described is compatible with another noble feeling, that of friendship.

A community of dangers, of glory, and of interest, establishes the strongest and most sincere ties, and as everything Is connected and bound together in the grand mystery of society, it is precisely in the time of war and in the midst of perils, that is to say, when society needs it most, that we find the greatest display of friendship, or that habit of comradeship—that *esprit de corps*, to which opinion has given so much strength.

An interchange of services rendered, a reciprocity of assistance received and given, doubles, nay, increases tenfold, the strength and the security of everyone. Thus opinion gives rise to, develops and exalts the virtues among men, just in proportion as circumstances render their display more necessary in the interest of the common preservation.

But the heart of man is very mobile, and the best sentiments are opposed by others which come from the same principle viewed from a different point I brave a great danger to save a comrade, because I expect he would do the like for me under similar circumstances; but should the immediate danger appear to me too great—should fear predominate over the interest that draws me towards the person threatened, the .instinct of my future preservation is effaced from my mind by the powerful sense of present peril; I recede from the danger, forgetful of all the motives that should have made me brave it. The feeling that sways me then, which is called fear, is by no means rare in the face of real danger; it is much more common, and exercises more influence than is generally believed in the great majority of persons. It is precisely in order to combat it, and in order to encourage opposite feelings that the power of discipline has been invoked to assist authority; and as example is potent in influencing the conduct of men, as the very brave often carry along the others, we cannot be too profuse in the rewards we bestow on those who prove themselves exceptions to the common rule, in order to exalt their generous dispositions, for on them often depends the fate of battles.

Bravery in the European armies of the present day, and particularly among the officers, may be thus classed:

The bravery that prevents a man incurring dishonour, that makes him do his duty strictly; this is not rare.

That which urges a man beyond duty; this is much less common.

Finally, that which induces a man to value his life infinitely less than the success of what is confided to him to prepare; this is rarest of all. So when such bravery is met with, honours, riches and applause should be its reward; and the opportunity of giving such recompenses, limited to such cases, is so rare, that it can never be a heavy expense to any state.

The feelings I have just mentioned should not be the only ones that ought to exist in the heart of the soldier. In order that troops should possess their full value, confidence should exist among those who compose an army. The private should believe in the bravery of his comrade. He will be convinced that his officer, while as brave as himself, is his superior in experience and education; he will attribute to his general the same bravery, and in addition science and talent. When such is the case, the army forms a bunch of faggots which no power can break. This is the foremost condition of the strength of armies, the foremost element of success.

But this fundamental basis, which we term confidence, is only possible in tried and veteran troops, and not in raw soldiers who do not know each other. Hence the absurdity of a national guard as a substitute for troops of the line. National guards, though they may be composed of the bravest men on earth, will be worth nothing at first starting; for the valour and capacity of each not being appreciated by the others, except by experience, the first efforts will be made without the aid of confidence, and will probably result in great and irreparable disasters.

The moral part of war, as far as the commander is concerned, consists in the knowledge of the mental emotions that animate soldiers; in the correctness of his judgment concerning them, and in the use he makes of these mental emotions in the varying chances of war in reference to his own troops, as well as those he has fought or means to fight. This is a faculty quite apart from professional skill, properly so called—it is an attribute of genius. All great commanders have possessed it, and none ever had it in a greater degree than Napoleon.

Discipline, the auxiliary of courage, is also necessary as a means of maintaining order. Its whole importance will be felt if we reflect on the mechanism of an army and consider how such a multitude is to live in movement as well as when at rest.

It is not sufficient to constitute an army to collect a larger or smaller number of men together; they must be also organised. I have explained above by what mechanism obedience is obtained, namely by putting those which are to command in the different ranks of the military hierarchy in contact with a limited number of men, on whom they may easily bring their faculties to bear. Once this division is effected and this organisation completed, we must concern ourselves with discipline, that is to say, accustom the subordinates to passive deference towards their superiors.

After that we come to the instruction of troops.

Thus, in order to form an assemblage of men into an army, three operations are required:—

1st. Organisation.
2nd. Discipline.
3rd. Instruction.

And the complement of these three is confidence: an essential element, without which an army loses most of its value. This confidence should extend to all, and to each; confidence of the soldiers in one another in their mutual relations; confidence of each soldier and officer in the superior officers, and especially in the chief of all.

This precious element, which acts so powerfully on the results, has an effect proportioned to the intelligence of the soldiers; for confidence, founded on the knowledge of men and things, is not an unintelligent feeling—a blind faith.

Soldiers without intelligence have little mobility, and vary less than those who are more lively and thoughtful The former are more easily commanded, and there is less risk in putting them under generals of limited capacity. The value of the latter, on the contrary, will be in proportion to the excellence of the genial who commands them.

When speaking of these kind of soldiers, I refer chiefly to the Germans and the French. The Germans are often successful with very second-rate chiefs. The French are ten times more valuable with a chief who possesses their love and esteem.

They will be utterly valueless under a chief who inspires neither esteem nor confidence. The truth of this was proved at Hochstett in 1704, before Turin in 1706, and at Vittoria in 1813. The reason is obvious. We do not go to war in order to be killed! Our object is always to conquer the enemy, and if we run the risk of being killed, it is on condition that the hypothetical sacrifice of life submitted to shall be of use. But should it so happen that an intelligent body of men have before them no probability of victory—no chance of a glorious fight, they will then hesitate to compromise their lives, and will try to preserve them for a time when they may be able to make a more useful sacrifice.

I have endeavoured to explain the various emotions that take place in the soldier's heart; emotions whence result phenomena of extraordinary character to the eyes of the ignorant, who, regarding men as mere passive machines, do not understand the variations to which they are liable. I shall now proceed to the questions of the command, and shall endeavour to show the qualities it requires.

The art of war is composed of two distinct parts, professional skill, properly so called, and moral qualities the attribute of genius. I have already developed my ideas concerning the moral qualities required in war, and I shall only add one word relative to the qualities which give to a chief authority over those around him.

First of all some individuals have the faculty of acting on the minds of others; they have a sort of natural authority which ensures to them a ready Obedience. This authority is a special gift, and depends on hidden causes which our minds cannot fathom. Thus one man who, having hitherto rendered obedience to others, is placed in command, and he wields the powers he is entrusted with from the very first with as much ease as if he had always possessed them. Another, and such cases are frequent, exercises over his equals an uncontested authority, though he may not have any right to it and is not even intellectually superior to those he sways; this faculty he derives from some peculiarity of organisation. The legitimate chief who possesses it inspires salutary fear. He is thought to be severe, and the severity attributed to him renders it unnecessary for him to exercise it. A look, a word acts on the minds of those under him with an irresistible ascendancy. Such men are destined by Providence to rule over others.

But as such natural power over one's fellows is rarely met with, subordinates have been prepared for obedience by being accustomed to pay respect and homage to their chiefs. Ranks have been established in order to determine the right of the command, and to maintain those invested with it in distinct and constant social positions. Public honours have been awarded to the highest ranks, in order to produce a striking effect on the imaginations.

In fine, nothing has been neglected that could tend to confer greatness on the depositories of power in the opinion of their subordinates so as the better to ensure their obedience, an easy enough matter in ordinary times and when there is nothing to prevent the preservation of regular order, but difficult indeed in the midst of dangers, sufferings and passions. When a general has a reputation for courage and ability, compelling esteem and securing confidence, his power is augmented; when to those qualities he adds the lustre of high birth, and an elevated social and domestic position, he seems to the multitude to be still greater. The more power and credit the depository of authority has, the more readily will his ability to distribute rewards be acknowledged, the more easy will it be for him to ensure obedience.

All these means united in the person of Napoleon contributed powerfully to his success. They compose, if I may so express myself, the conditions required for command. But what are the personal qualities required for command? (See note following).

Note:—I have established above the conditions most favourable to command, and it follows that when the general is at the same time the sovereign he is greatly aided by this relation to his subordinates:—absolute liberty in his schemes, movements, and operations; accumulation of means and resources; absence of responsibility; the faculty of carrying out hazardous combinations, which, though attended by great risks, promise great advantages if successful; certainty of being always obeyed, whatever happens, and served with zeal, &c.

In contrast with a position so advantageous, a mere general has very limited means at his command. Whatever powers he may possess, they have always certain limits. It is not sufficient that he does well, but he must also be prepared to justify his undertakings. Finally, doubts may be cast on the obedience due to him; rivalries, hatred, intrigues, &c., may be powerful auxiliaries of the enemy he has to fight.

These two situations admit of no comparison; and the merit of the successful General is much greater than that of the Sovereign. Accordingly the glory of Napoleon in Germany is not by any means equal to that of General Bonaparte in Italy. In his first campaign, without a name, without experience in command, with feeble, imperfect means, an inferior, ill-provided army, he obtained brilliant successes, conquered and retained possession of Italy. In his other campaigns, apart from the splendid combinations they developed, the vastness of the means employed and accumulated, the abundance of the resources of all kinds seem to exempt genius from the trouble of securing the almost inevitable victory.

The chances of success being more numerous for the military monarch than for the simple general, one might conclude that it were desirable that the former took the command, and yet the reverse is the case.

And, first, who can be a competent judge of the talents of the sovereign? And who can guarantee that his illusions regarding his own abilities shall not inspire him with a fatal confidence? Even supposing he does not assume the chief part until after numerous essays, there will still always be great danger to the state; for reverses mil produce an unfavourable effect in public opinion on the consideration to the principle of kingly power, which would be an immense social misfortune. Moreover, the command of armies requires, in the interest of the public, to be subjected to control. Whatever be the latitude allowed a chief, there are limits which he should not pass; and if he is uncontrolled, who shall guarantee his moderation in the chances he would run?

The greatness of catastrophes is always in proportion to the accumulation of means and the extent of the enterprise; and when these are vast, society is shaken to its very basis. The faults or misfortunes of a general are always reparable in a great country; those of a sovereign of exalted imagination bring about his complete ruin. Therefore the sovereign should confine himself to governing, administering, creating means and make them abundant fie should, moreover, give his full confidence to him who is worthy of it, and reward with magnificence and without jealousy; but he should never assume the responsibility and the burden of the command.

The art of war, considered in a professional point of view, is a mere matter of combinations and calculation. I have entered into circumstantial details on this view of the subject when treating of strategy and tactics. But in order that favourable results should ensue from the combinations, it is necessary that a strong will should dominate; for changes in plans fixed or without due deliberation are attended by many inconveniences, and often cause great misfortunes.

Two things are required in a general, intellect and character. Intellect, for without that one can form no combinations, but must give in without defence. Character, for without a strong and persistent will, it is impossible to secure the execution of plans resolved on. But it is here relative qualities are superior to absolute qualities, and character must dominate intellect. It is in this relation that the elements of success is to be found. Supposing we were to estimate in figures each of these faculties, I would rather that a general had intellect = 5, and character = 10, than intellect = 15, and character = 8. When the character dominates the intellect, and the latter is of a certain calibre, we shall proceed towards a certain aim with the chance of reaching it. When intellect dominates character, we are constantly changing our opinions, projects and direction, for a mighty intellect sees questions at every moment in a new light. If strength of will does not guard us against such changes, we become distracted with the multitude of views of the question; we fail to embrace any one, consequently, and instead of approaching the aim, the uncertainty of our efforts often reverses us still farther from it.

Still we should do very wrong to suppose that a great deal of intellect is not required in order to prepare grand actions. We see no mediocrity of intellect in any of the great generals of antiquity and of modern times, in any of those historical names that surge out in byegone ages above all the others. Alexander, Hannibal, Scipio, Caesar possessed the highest faculties of mind. The same was the case with the great Condé, Luxembourg, the great Eugène, Frederic, and Napoleon. But all these illustrious men, while endowed with superior intellect, possessed character in a still greater degree.

This necessity for intellect in subjection to character is felt each moment by every commander, for in that capacity there is frequent occasion for forming a resolution and deciding on a plan. Now, what men of feeble character dread most is to form a resolution; an unfortunate instinct impels them frequently to make a decision when it is of the most urgent importance to do so, and when at last it is made, it is no longer useful, sometimes, indeed, disastrous, in consequence of the delay.

This truth authorises me to proclaim the following maxims:—a general may take advice when he feels the need of it, but the part of habitual adviser, unless it be promoted by the supreme chief, cannot be successfully enacted.

The necessity for rapidly forming resolutions is the difficulty of command. It is at that moment that responsibility, with all its important accompaniments, presents itself with all the interests we are charged with, and which we heartily wish to defend; responsibility towards those on whom we depend; responsibility towards public opinion; responsibility towards ourselves, towards our conscience; altogether an immense responsibility; the more terrible the more desirous we are of doing our duty.

There is but one mode of supporting the burden: to have sufficient strength and resolution to place ourselves above all the consequences, certain of finding in our consciences and our intentions a generous approval of what we have done, after having applied to the task all our faculties and all our intelligence. But few men are able to place themselves at this height This necessity for deciding on our plans, is at once so important and so difficult for the command, that when the resolution taken is of an unalterable character, and when the cannon roars, when the battle has commenced, when each has had indicated to him the part he has to play, the Supreme Chief is tranquil, he has recovered the serenity and repose of mind of which he was previously deprived.

Thus, then, when a general possesses intellect to see, judge and combine, and character to execute; when to these gifts is joined a knowledge of men, of the passions that sway them and of the secret emotions of their hearts which so many causes develop in war; when, moreover, the danger so far from depriving him of his faculties only increases and energizes them; when, in fine, he loves his soldiers, is loved by them, and is anxious for their preservation, their interests and their well-being, like a father of a family; then and then only does he unite all the qualities that promise success. I say promise and not ensure, for war has such a variety of chances and so many risks, that nothing is certain before the event is actually accomplished. When treating of the qualities required for the exercise of the command, I meant the chief command.

Any other command, however extensive it may be, cannot, inasmuch as it is subordinate, be at all compared with the commander-in-chief, however limited the latter may be by the small number of troops; for the great difficulty I have sought to explain, the forming of resolutions, has not to be surmounted. Under Napoleon, I have commanded armies of various strengths and *corps d'armée*. To command only 10,000 men as absolute chief, gives much more trouble than the command of 50,000 men, as a portion of an army of 200,000. In the latter case, to move, to march and to fight in obedience to orders given and to effect an end indicated, are easy matters; and when the battle or the march is over, when the camp is pitched, the general rests like the meanest soldier, waiting for his orders; whilst, on the contrary, that is precisely the moment when the Supreme Chief is more subject to anxiety and engaged in forming all sorts of plans.

CHAPTER 3

Portrait of a General Who Possesses All the Qualities Required For the Command

I shall sum up here in a few words the qualities required by a general called to the command.

He is brave, and acknowledged to be so by the whole army. His courage cannot be for one moment questioned or doubted. His bravery is calm and cool in character, and in certain circumstances it possesses that power and energy that are infectious, and carry all along with them. If his reputation on this point is not sufficiently established, he ought to watch for and seize on the opportunity for establishing it incontrovertibly; otherwise, he will never be able to exercise over the generals, officers and soldiers, that power of respect and esteem that are indispensable to success.

When once his reputation is made he will avoid uselessly risking his life, without, however, displaying too great a solicitude about it.

His mind, as I have said before, is subordinate to his character.

His physical powers are able to resist the greatest fatigues; and considerations of health never prevent him seeing for himself everything of importance; and the best drawn up reports—the account given by the ablest persons—can never give that precise knowledge which he would obtain by personal inspection.

If nature has endowed him with high faculties it is desirable that he should obtain the command early in life. His success will thereby be rendered more certain. He will have that marvellous energy and that confidence in himself that will double his powers—an object of sympathy for all the youth of the army. He will at the same time show great deference for age, and will be endowed personally with sufficient experience. There are certain things that time and use alone can teach that do not come by intuition. But habits of obedience practised too long diminish rather than develop the faculties of command.

Above all things, it is necessary that he shall have been actually engaged in war while yet very young, and soon after his adoption of a military career; otherwise, he will, with difficulty, acquire that tact and that instinct which war creates, and which greatly simplify its difficulties.

He will always be impressed with the belief that one can never be surprised unless one has been guilty of culpable negligence, and that a general surprised is dishonoured. It is not himself only, it is all his subordinates whom he must secure from all reproach, by guarding against their faults.

Knowing the value of time—the only treasure that cannot be replaced—he will avoid writing much himself, and will leave this task to those whose duty it is to transmit his orders. He will merely reserve to himself the care of supervising their composition. No good general ever yet wrote much during the actual operations of war. It is the head, not the hand that should work. His time is more usefully employed in giving verbal instructions—in preserving his freedom of mind in order to judge if his intentions have been correctly rendered, and to plan new combinations. His activity should be incessant; by appearing in different places unexpectedly, he will inspire all with a wholesome fear of any dereliction of duty; thus he will ensure its zealous performance by all.

In all his decisions he will be guided by impartial justice, severity in the maintenance of order and discipline, and security to the soldiers of the enjoyment of their rights and the greatest amount of comfort compatible with their situation.

If severity is one of his duties, he has another much more pleasant but not less important: I allude to rewards due to distinguished actions and good conduct. Of these he should be neither prodigal nor niggardly; he should make it his own business to obtain them, displaying more eagerness about them than if they were for himself; he should take care that the right to the reward be founded on real merit; for if a just recompense encourages generous hearts, an unmerited reward destroys all emulation and fosters intrigue. The instinct of man and his innate love of justice always enlighten him as to the spirit that presides over the distribution of rewards.

If the general be faithful to those principles, if he fulfil the conditions I have enumerated, he will be the object of the respect, the esteem and the affection of his troops. The necessity of order is felt so deeply by soldiers that they love severity in a chief because it guarantees order; and they confidently rely on one whose decisions will, they are sure, be accompanied by firmness and equity.

Amiability without strength is of no use; it is believed, and with reason, to be akin to the weakness that leads a chief to be swayed by those around him. But amiability united to a judicious severity makes a general the idol of his soldiers. Rigour of whatever degree demands forms and should never be accompanied by insult; we resign ourselves to deserved punishment, but insult irritates. A just punishment produces all the greater effect if it is inflicted with the utmost calmness; violence in a chief justifies the murmur of a culpable subordinate. Besides a general should always treat with consideration every one who wears a soldier's uniform.

There is something so noble in the profession of arms, the sacrifice of life is so sublime; that those who are always ready to offer it have a right to consideration even when they deserve an act of severity. A general should be of habitually grave manners in his communications with his subordinates; and still the authority he exercises should not prevent a kind of familiarity, of that dignified gaiety which inspires affection and esteem. There is a sentiment of brotherhood which a community of dangers, privations, and toils naturally engenders among military men, and which has nothing incompatible with the rules of the hierarchy and the maintenance of discipline. The more a general forgets his superiority, the less apt is the soldier to do so. A general should be accessible to every one.

He should receive and open at the instant any dispatch that is brought to him, and not defer doing so from any motives of personal comfort. In the midst of the fatigues of a campaign, though he may have been roused twenty times in one night for unimportant news, he will not give orders not to be again disturbed. Tidings during war may be of such importance, and a delay of a couple hours be so disastrous, that the fate of an army may depend on them.

A general should live as expensively as his fortune will allow him. His first luxury should be a large stud of horses; he must have a sufficient number, so as never to be prevented taking any rides he may deem necessary. The next piece of luxury he should indulge in is a house in which he may continually exercise hospitality. No officer should ever come to see him about the affairs of the campaign without partaking of it. In the first place it is a laudable act in itself; for officers of the staff, or officers at a distance from their corps, are so badly off for the means of living, that unless the generals are careful they may be reduced to real privations.

In addition to this consideration of humanity, there is something that concerns the interests of the service itself. An officer charged with a mission hastens his arrival when he knows beforehand that he will be well received. Affection for his chief and for himself makes him get over his journey quickly. Time, always valuable, is particularly so in war, and should be economised in every possible way.

A general should avail himself of every means of making himself minutely acquainted beforehand with the country where he is going to fight. He will procure all kinds of statistical information respecting it: he will learn what are its resources of all sorts, and carefully study its topography. The slightest error in this study may be fraught with the most serious consequences. Too much consideration cannot be bestowed on the circumstances that characterise a country and the best means of utilizing them. The best map should be procured, and should be incessantly looked at; even though this is done sometime in a vague manner, yet one is sure to acquire notions, sometimes happy ones and of great value when applied.

Insufficient information almost proved fatal in the immortal campaign of Marengo in 1800, at its very commencement, and was the cause of many difficulties. The First Consul did not know of the existence of the Fort of Bard and its means of resistance: it would have been easy for us to have carried it, had we brought sufficiently heavy pieces of ordnance along with the first troops. It was not known that the little St. Bernard which, like the great St Bernard, leads into the valley of Aosta, was practicable for artillery; the passage of the mountains would have been more speedily accomplished, and would not have presented all those obstacles which made it one of the most remarkable operations of modern times.

All projects demand the most profound secrecy; a general should only communicate them to those entrusted with their execution, and at the very instant when it is necessary they should be known. How many enterprises, well planned, have failed in consequence of becoming known to the enemy! On the other hand, nothing is more conducive to success than to allow people to imagine something the very opposite of what we are going to do; it is by deceiving those around him that the general most surely disconcerts the enemy.

But while he carefully conceals his own projects, he should endeavour to ascertain those of his adversaries; he should neglect nothing for this object. Without having a blind faith in spies, he should treat and pay them well. It is especially useful to establish intelligence with the *employés* attached to the staff.

Should he succeed in doing so, one of his first cares should be to obtain a detailed account of the organisation of the different corps composing the enemy's army, with the names of the generals in command of them. With this assistance, and with light troops, well officered, constantly hovering about the enemy and making prisoners, he will always possess reliable data respecting the movements about to take place. The capture of a single soldier of a certain regiment shows the presence of a certain division belonging to a certain corps, and from this a general will be able to see what are the intentions, what the object of his adversary's manoeuvres and operations. One would scarcely imagine the candour, simplicity and truth with which a prisoner will answer questions without a suspicion of their object, and without the faintest idea of damaging the cause he has zealously served, and which he would never dream of betraying.

Finally, the general who is concerned for his reputation, ought to liberate himself in his operations from absolute dependence; it is always pernicious. An enlightened government makes no pretensions to direct everything; it confines itself to indicating the object to be attained, after having determined the nature of the means and the amount available. To the general who is placed face to face with and in the midst of the difficulties, it must be left to decide on the system to be pursued and the combinations to be executed. Rather than submit to a too direct action on the part of the government, the general should resign a command he cannot fully exercise: if he does so, either the government will cease to thwart him if he still retains its confidence, or it will accept his resignation, if it believes he is pursuing a wrong course.

Government should not act on a general who possesses its confidence, save by the influence of advice which has not the character of imperative commands; it should refrain from imposing on him an official counsellor, for nothing can be more absurd than such a system, and, as I have said before, its results are always disastrous. A general may promote discussions, consult men of enlightenment, and even .adopt their advice when he thinks it useful; but he should not be obliged to ask or fellow anyone's advice. In the army, as a role, there are only two parts to be played—to obey or to command. The government should give the command of its armies to those it thinks most worthy, and at the same time should grant them its unreserved confidence: unless it can do so, it should appoint others.

CHAPTER 4.

On the Reputation of Generals

I shall conclude this work with some reflections on the reputation of generals, and the causes that should lead to its establishment.

Generals sometimes contrive to attach their names to successes which were not owing to them; successes obtained in spite of their arrangements, or in consequence of advice given them, and happily followed by them.

I have known several examples of this: the most notable is the case of Marshal Brune,[1] who in every respect was a very second-rate man. And yet his name is associated with three glorious reminiscences; with the success of the French army against the Swiss in 1798; against the English and Russians in 1799; against the Austrians in Italy in 1800.

In Switzerland, the superiority of our forces and the divisions existing in that country necessarily won one triumph. In Holland, he was not at the Battle of Berghen; the Battle of Bewervich was brought on accidentally, without plan and without direction; the folly and stupidity of the Duke of York brought about the result. In 1800, in Italy, after brilliant successes with which the commander-in-chief had almost nothing to do, we were in a position, if we had had a different sort of man at our head, utterly to destroy the enemy's army.

I might adduce examples of a contrary character, that is to say, where the efforts of men of great talent have been thwarted by fortune.

But these examples should not prevent us judging by the results, and this is the fairest way of appreciating the worth and merit of generals. To adopt any other basis, to rest our judgment on the idea

1. In spite of excellent private qualities, and the deplorable end he met with, we cannot help acknowledging that Marshal Brune was one of the most singular and striking examples of the caprices of fortune.

we may have formed of the intelligence and talents of a general, is to involve ourselves in an inextricable labyrinth, and run the risk of committing great mistakes, for each will only see through the prism of prejudice, friendship and passion. If we sometimes make mistakes when judging after the facts, we should make still greater mistakes were we to be guided solely by personal acquaintance with the individuals judged of. Fortune may once or twice shower her favours on an unworthy man; she may thwart the highest combinations of genius and bring humiliation on a noble brow; but when the strife is prolonged, and a series of events occur, the best man will inevitably prevail. If defeat follows defeat continually, you may conclude, in spite of the superior intellect and dazzling qualities, that a want of harmony among the faculties destroys their power.

I may class generals in four categories.

In the first, I shall place the generals who have won all the battles they have fought. They occupy incontestably the first place in public estimation. But their number is so small that scarcely one can be named. In antiquity I see none besides Alexander and Caesar. The Greek generals, who bear an illustrious reputation like Miltiades and Epaminondas, owed all their fame to one or two battles.

In modern times, I only see Gustavus Adolphus, Turenne, Condé, Luxembourg and Napoleon, until 1812, for I am justified in reckoning among the disasters for which a general is responsible the destruction of armies caused by a want of care and excessive improvidence.

In the second category, I would place those generals who, though they often gained battles, yet sometimes lost them after a hard conflict. This includes most of those whose names are inscribed in the temple of fame. Perhaps some of them are worthy of figuring in the preceding class. For, suppose two generals fighting with equal skill, victory must remain to one of them, but it will have been dearly bought, and its consequences will be trifling.

In the third category will be those generals who, usually unfortunate in war, and meeting with frequent defeats, have never been utterly discomfited nor discouraged, but have always been able to make themselves threatening and formidable to the enemy.

Such generals are rare; and they must exercise a great ascendancy on those around them. Such were Sertorius and Mithridates in ancient times; such were Wallenstein and William III. of England in modern times.

Finally, in the fourth category, will naturally be found those who lose their armies without fighting, or without making the enemy pay dearly for his victory by a vigorous resistance. It would be easy to give a long list of such generals. Every country—every age can show specimens of them.

Conclusion

From all the foregoing remarks I think I may draw the following conclusions:—

1st. The fundamental principle of the organisation of an army is in the fact and the spirit of aggregation of an assemblage of men which becomes a compact mass, a unit, to the different parts of which an able and ingenious mechanism gives great mobility.

2nd. The parts that go to make up the elements of this whole ought to have dimensions—a form and limits, which are the necessary consequence of the faculties of man and of the arms he employs.

3rd. There is nothing arbitrary in the organisation of troops and the movements of armies. On the contrary everything connected with them ought to depend on roles themselves derived from certain laws. To make a proper application of them constitutes the totality of military science.

4th. An army is composed of material and men. There are natural fixed relations between these two elements, varying, however, according to circumstances, and to the object aimed at. These relative proportions do not depend on caprice, but solely on the nature of things.

5th. The goodness or badness of the elements has a powerful influence on the results, and here quantity is of much less importance than quality.

6th. A third element affects the value of an army; I mean the moral element It alone is often of more importance than the others, provided the latter have a certain degree of effective power; for there must be a body for the spirit to animate. Thus, up to a certain pointy the real strength of an army is not increased in proportion to the number of soldiers and material means, but it may be vastly increased according to the spirit that animates it.

7th, To develop the spirit of an army, to augment its confidence, to appeal to its imagination, and to exalt the soul of the soldier, should be the constant aim of the general.

8th. The element of military spirit is "*esprit de corps.*" It is a powerful spring that cannot be too highly encouraged. It should be the conviction of every soldier that the army he belongs to and his general are invincible; that his division is the best in the army, and his regiment the bravest and most distinguished. This conviction will increase tenfold his strength and his courage.

9th. Finally, every warrior should be deeply impressed with a concern for the glory of his country and with loyalty to his prince, which is its representative and expression. Love of country, that divine sentiment graven by Providence in the hearts of all men, should constantly sustain him, exalt him, and keep him up to the height of circumstances. But this sentiment should not be an empty word; it must be sincere, serious, and energetic; its reality should be proved, when necessary, by any sacrifice. The history of all times records instances of this, rare, no doubt, but sublime, the results of which have astonished the world.

10th. The best army is that which most completely fulfils the above conditions; it is their assemblage and their harmony that constitute its real value. As these conditions are almost all variable and difficult to be appreciated, since the mind cannot grasp all possible combinations, no one can determine accurately beforehand the effective power of an army; we judge of it only by a sort of instinct which is not far from the truth. But afterwards we can accurately estimate its value by the nature of its actions and their results.

I now conclude this sketch, which will suffice to effect the object I had in view. To give to each of its component parts the development it admits of would require a much larger work, which I have neither the strength nor the wish to undertake. I have said enough on the subject to give rise to reflection, and to demonstrate that our sublime profession is based on principles which should never be departed from; which, when attended to, give to the means of action at our disposal their utmost possible value; and this should be the constant aim of every commander.

Auguste de Marmont, Duke of Ragusa

Auguste Frédéric Louis Viesse De Marmont, the youngest of Napoleon's Marshals, was born at Châtillon-sur-Seine on July 25, 1774. The family of Viesse belonged to the smaller nobility, who from the days of Richelieu had supplied the officers of the line for the old royal army. Marmont's father had destined him from the cradle for the military career, and had devoted his life to training him, both in body and mind, for the profession of arms. His hours of patience and self-denial were not thrown away, for, thanks to his early Spartan training, the Duke of Ragusa seldom knew fatigue or sickness, and owing to this physical strength was able, without neglecting his professional duties, to spend hours on scientific and literary work.

In 1792 young Marmont, at the age of eighteen, passed the entrance examination for the Artillery School at Châlons, and started his military career with his father's oft-repeated words ringing in his ears, "Merit without success is infinitely better than success without merit, but determination and merit always command success."

The young artillery cadet had both determination and capacity and his early career foreshadowed his future success. Aristocratic to the bone, Marmont detested the excesses of the Revolution; but politics, during his early years, had little effect on his thoughts, which were solely fixed on military glory. The exigencies of the revolutionary wars cut short his student days at Châlons, and before the end of 1792 he was gazetted to the first artillery regiment. In February, 1793, he saw his first active service with the Army of the Alps, under General Kellermann. Owing to the dearth of trained officers, though only newly gazetted, he performed all the duties of a senior colonel, laying out entrenched camps and commanding the artillery of the division to

which he was attached. It was with this promising record already behind him that he attracted Bonaparte's attention at the siege of Toulon
by his admirable handling of the guns under his command, and by
his inventive powers, which overcame all obstacles. From that day the
Corsican destined him for his service, and during the campaign in the
Maritime Alps used him as an unofficial *aide-de-camp*. So devoted did
Marmont become to the future emperor, that when Bonaparte was
arrested at the time of Robespierre's fall, he and Junot formed a plan
of rescuing their idol by killing the sentries and carrying him off by
sea.

When Bonaparte returned to Paris Marmont accompanied him,
and was offered the post of superintendent of the gun factory at
Moulins. He contemptuously refused this position, telling the inspector of ordnance that he would not mind such a post in peace time, but
that he was going to see as much active service as he could while the
war lasted, so at his own request he was posted to the army of Piche-
gru, which was besieging Maintz. A temporary suspension of hostili-
ties on the Rhine gave him the opportunity of once again joining his
chosen leader, and early in 1796 he started for Italy on Bonaparte's
staff. Lodi was one of the great days of his life. Early in the action he
captured one of the enemy's batteries, but a moment later he was
thrown from his horse and ridden over by the whole of the cavalry,
without, however, receiving a single scratch.

Scarcely had he mounted when he was despatched along the river,
under fire of the whole Austrian force on the other bank, to carry
orders to the commander of the cavalry, who was engaged in fording
the river higher up. Of his escort of five, two were killed, while his
horse was severely wounded, yet he managed to return in time to take
his place among the band of heroes who forced the long bridge in the
face of a storm of bullets and grape. Castiglione added to his laurels,
for it was his handling of the artillery that enabled Augereau to win
his great victory. The marshal, in his *Memoirs*, asserts that this short
campaign was the severest strain he ever underwent.

I never at any other time endured such fatigue as during the eight
days of that campaign. Always on horseback, on reconnaissance, or
fighting, I was, I believe, five days without sleep, save for a few sto-
len minutes. After the final battle the general-in-chief gave me leave
to rest and I took full advantage of it. I ate, I lay down, and I slept
twenty-four hours at a stretch, and, thanks to youth, hardiness, a good
constitution, and the restorative powers of sleep, I was as fresh again as

at the beginning of the campaign.

Though Castiglione thus brought him fresh honours, it nearly caused an estrangement between him and his chief. For Bonaparte, ever with an eye to the future, desiring to gain as many friends as possible, chose one of Berthier's staff officers to take the news of the victory to Paris. This was a bitter blow to his ambitious *aide-de-camp*, whose pride was further piqued because his hero, forgetting that he had not to deal with one of the ordinary adventurers who formed so large a number of the officers of the Army of Italy, with great want of tact, had offered him opportunities of adding to his wealth by perquisites and commissions abhorrent to the eyes of a descendant of an honourable family. But the exigencies of war and the thirst for glory left little time for brooding, and Bonaparte, recognising with whom he had to deal, took the opportunity of the successful fighting which penned Würmser into Mantua to send Marmont with despatches to Paris.

As his reward the Minister of War promoted him colonel and commandant of the second regiment of horse artillery. A curious state of affairs arose from this appointment, for promotion in the artillery ran quite independent of ordinary army rank. Accordingly, the army list ran as follows: Bonaparte, lieutenant-colonel of a battalion of artillery, seconded as general-in-chief of the Army of Italy. Marmont, colonel of the second regiment horse artillery, seconded as *aide-de-camp* to Lieutenant-Colonel Bonaparte, the commander-in-chief of the Army of Italy.

Marmont hurried back to Italy in time to join Bonaparte's staff an hour before the battle of Arcola. The Austrians were making their last effort to relieve the fortress of Mantua, and it seemed as if they would be successful, as Alvinzi had concentrated forty thousand troops against twenty-six thousand. The French attempted a surprise, but were discovered, and for three days the fate of the campaign hung on the stubborn fight in the marshes of Arcola. It was Marmont who helped to extricate Bonaparte when he was flung off the embankment into the ditch, a service which Bonaparte never forgot. Diplomatic missions to Venice and the Vatican slightly turned the young soldier's head, and his chief had soon to give him a severe reprimand for loitering among Josephine's beauties at Milan instead of hastening back to headquarters. But to a man of Marmont's character one word of warning was enough; his head governed his heart; glory was his loadstar. Ambitious though he was, he was essentially a man of honour and fine feelings, and refused the hand of Pauline Bonaparte for the simple reason that he did not truly love her.

A year later he made a love match with Mademoiselle Perrégaux, but differences of temperament and the long separation which his military career imposed caused the marriage to turn out unhappily, and this lack of domestic felicity spoiled the marshal's life and nearly embittered his whole character, turning him for the time into a self-centred man with an eye solely to his own glory and a sharp tongue which did not spare even his own friends. Yet in his early days Marmont was a bright and cheerful companion and no one enjoyed more a practical joke, getting up sham duels between cowards or sending bogus instructions to officious commanders. But fond as he was of amusement, even during his early career he could find delight in the society of men of science and learning like Monge and Berthollet.

After the peace of Campo Formio he accompanied his chief to Paris, where an incident occurred which illustrates well the character of the two men. The Minister of War wanted detailed information regarding the English preparations against invasion, and Bonaparte offered to send his *aide-de-camp* as a spy. Marmont indignantly refused to go in such a capacity, and a permanent estrangement nearly took place. Their standards had nothing in common; in the one honour could conquer ambition, in the other ambition knew no rules of honour.

However, their lust for glory brought them together again, and Marmont sailed with the Egyptian expedition. He was despatched north to command Alexandria after the battle of the Pyramids, where his guns had played so important a part in shattering the Mamelukes. Later he was entrusted with the control of the whole of the Mediterranean littoral. His task was a difficult one, but a most useful training for a young commander. With a tiny garrison he had to hold the important town of Alexandria and to keep in order a large province; to organise small columns to repress local risings; to make his own arrangements for raising money to pay his troops, and consequently to reorganise the fiscal system of the country; to reconstruct canals and to improvise flotillas of barges to supply Alexandria with provisions; to keep in touch with the remnant of the French fleet and thus to try to establish communications with Europe. He was responsible for resisting any attempt at invasion by the Turks or the English, and it was mainly owing to his measures that when the former landed at Aboukir they were destroyed before they could march inland. While his comrades were gaining military glory in Syria, he was fighting the plague at Alexandria, learning that patient attention to detail and careful supervision of the health of his troops were as important attributes of a commander as dash and courage in the field.

Marmont quitted Egypt with joy; he had learned many useful lessons, but, like the rest of the army, he hated the country and the half Oriental life, and above all, as he said, "seeing a campaign and not taking part in it was a horrible punishment." On returning to Paris his time was fully occupied in winning over the artillery to Bonaparte. He had no false ideas on the subject, for, as he said to Junot before the Egyptian expedition, "You will see, my friend, that on his return Bonaparte will seize the crown."

As his reward the First Consul gave him the choice of the command of the artillery of the Guard or a seat as Councillor of State. Jealous of Lannes, and flattered by the title, he chose the councillorship, in which capacity he was employed on the War Committee and entrusted with the reorganisation of the artillery. His first business was to provide a proper train to ensure the quick and easy mobilisation of the artillery. After the Marengo campaign he took in hand the reform of the *matériel*. Too many different types of guns existed. Marmont reorganised both the field and the fortress artillery, replacing the seven old types of guns by three—namely, six-pounders, twelve-pounders and twenty-four pounders; he also reduced the different types of wheels for gun carriages, limbers and wagons from twenty-four to eight, thus greatly simplifying the provision of ammunition and the work of repair in the field.

The Marengo campaign added to his prestige as an artillery officer. It was owing to his ingenuity that the guns were unmounted and pulled by hand in cradles up the steep side of the mountain and thus safely taken over the St. Bernard Pass. It was his ingenious brain which suggested the paving of the road with straw, whereby the much-needed artillery was forwarded to Lannes by night, without any casualties, right under the batteries of the fortress of Bard. It was owing to his foresight that the reserve battery of guns, captured from the enemy, saved the day at Marengo by containing the Austrians while Desaix's fresh troops were being deployed, and it was the tremendous effect of his massed battery which gave Kellermann the opportunity for his celebrated charge. The First Consul marked his approval by promoting Marmont a general of division, and thus at the age of twenty-six the young artillery officer had nearly reached the head of his profession.

After Marengo he continued his work of reorganisation, but before the end of the year he was once again in Italy, this time as a divisional commander under Brune, who, being no great strategist, was glad to avail himself of the brains of the First Consul's favourite: it was thanks to Marmont's plans that the French army successfully crossed the Mincio in the face of the enemy and, forced on him the armistice of Treviso. When Moreau's victory of Hohenlinden induced Austria to make peace, the general was sent to reorganise the Italian artillery on the same principles he had laid down for the French. He established an immense foundry and arsenal at Pavia, and the excellence of his plans was clearly proved in many a later campaign. From Italy he was recalled to Paris in September, 1802, as inspector-general of artillery. He threw himself heart and soul into his new duties, but found time to increase his scientific knowledge and to keep himself up to date with everything in the political and scientific world. He keenly supported Fulton's invention of the steamboat, and pressed it on the First Consul, and to the day of his death he was convinced that, if the emperor had adopted the invention, the invasion of England would have been successful.

The year 1804 brought him the delight of his first important command. In February he was appointed chief of the corps of the Army of the Ocean which was stationed in Holland. He entered on his task with his usual fervour. His first step was to make friends with all the Dutch officials, and thus to secure the smooth working of his commissariat and supply departments; then he turned to the actual training of his troops. For this purpose he obtained permission to hold a big camp of instruction, where all the divisions of his corps were massed. So successful was this experiment that it became an annual institution. But amid all the pleasure of this congenial work came the bitter moment when he found the name of so mediocre a soldier as Bessières included in the list of the new marshals and his own omitted. It was a sore blow, and his appointment as colonel-general of the horse chasseurs and Grand Eagle of the Legion of Honour did little to mitigate it. The emperor, careful as ever to stimulate devotion, later explained to him that a dashing officer like himself would have plenty of opportunities of gaining distinction, while this was Bessières's only chance. But in spite of this the neglect rankled, and from that day he was no longer the blindly devoted follower of Napoleon.

On the outbreak of the Austrian War Marmont's corps became the second corps of the Grand Army. In the operations ending in Ulm the second corps formed part of the left wing. After the capitulation it was detached to cover the French communications from an attack from the direction of Styria. In the summer of the following year Marmont was despatched as commander-in-chief to Dalmatia, where he spent the next five years of his life. Dalmatia had been ceded to France by the treaty of Pressburg. In Napoleon's eyes the importance of the province lay in the harbour of Cattaro, which he regarded as an outlet to the Balkan Peninsula. His intention was to get possession of Montenegro, to come to an understanding with Ali Pacha of Janina and the Sultan, and oppose the policy of Russia. But the Russians and Montenegrins had seized Cattaro, and were threatening to besiege Ragusa. It was to meet this situation that the emperor in July, 1806, hastily sent his former favourite to Dalmatia. The new commander-in-chief found himself, as in Egypt, faced with the difficulty of supply. Half the army was in hospital from want of proper nourishment and commonsense sanitation. Having, by his care of his men, refilled his battalions, he advanced boldly on the enemy, and drove them out of their positions. This punishment kept the Montenegrins quiet for the future, and the Russians fell back on Cattaro.

From there he was unable to drive them owing to the guns of their fleet, and it was not till the treaty of Tilsit that the French got possession of the coveted port. The French commander's chief difficulty in administering his province was that which is felt in all uncivilised countries, the difficulty of holding down a hostile population where roads do not exist. Otherwise his just but stern rule admirably suited the townsmen of the little cities on the coast, while order was kept among the hill tribes by making their headmen responsible for their behaviour, and by aiding them in attacking the Turks, who had seized certain tracts of territory and maltreated the inhabitants. But it was not gratitude which kept the hill-men quiet, so much as the miles of new roads on which the French commander employed his army when not engaged on expeditions against restless marauders.

During his years in the Dalmatian provinces Marmont constructed more than two hundred miles of roads, with the result that his small force was able with ease to hold down the long narrow mountainous province by the speed with which he could mobilise his punitive expeditions. Moreover, owing to the increased means of traffic the peasants were able to find a market for their goods, and the prosperity of the country increased beyond belief. With prosperity came contentment: manufactures were established, and the mines and the other natural resources of the country were exploited to advantage. As the emperor of Austria said to Metternich in 1817, when visiting the province, "It is a great pity that Marshal Marmont was not two or three years longer in Dalmatia."

The years spent at Ragusa were probably the happiest of Marmont's life. His successful work was recognised in 1808, when the emperor created him Duke of Ragusa. Each day was full of interest. He was head of the civil administration and of the judicial and fiscal departments. As commander-in-chief he was responsible for the health, welfare, and discipline of the troops, and for the military works which were being erected to protect the province from Austrian aggression. He had his special hobby—the roads. Yet in spite of all this business he found time to put himself in the hands of a tutor and to work ten hours a day at history, chemistry, and anatomy. To aid him in his studies he collected a travelling library of six hundred volumes which accompanied him in all his later campaigns.

The Austrian campaign of 1809 called him from these congenial labours to the even more congenial operations of war. The duty of the Army of Dalmatia was to attempt to cut off the Archduke John on his retirement from Italy; but the Duke of Ragusa had not sufficient troops to carry out this operation successfully, although he effected a junction with the Army of Italy. After a succession of small engagements the united armies found themselves on the Danube in time to take part in the battle of Wagram. In reserve during the greater part of the battle, Marmont's corps was entrusted with the pursuit of the enemy.

Unfortunately, either from lack of appreciation of the situation or from jealousy, their commander refused to allow Davout to co-operate with him, and consequently, although he overtook the Austrians, he was not strong enough to hold them till other divisions of the army came up. However, at the end of the operations Napoleon created him Marshal. But the Duke of Ragusa's joy at receiving this gift was tempered by the way it was given. For the emperor, angry doubtless at the escape of the Austrians, told him, "I have given you your nomination and I have great pleasure in bestowing on you this proof of my affection, but I am afraid I have incurred the reproach of listening rather to my affection than to your right to this distinction. You have plenty of intelligence, but there are needed for war qualities in which you are still lacking, and which you must work to acquire. Between ourselves, you have not yet done enough to justify entirely my choice. At the same time, I am confident that I shall have reason to congratulate myself on having nominated you, and that you will justify me in the eyes of the army."

Unkind critics of the three new marshals created after Wagram said that Napoleon, having lost Lannes, wanted to get the small change for him, but it is only fair to remember that though Macdonald, Marmont, and Oudinot were all inferior to Lannes, they were quite as good soldiers as some of the original marshals.

After peace was declared the new marshal returned to Dalmatia and took up the threads of his old life. He had won the respect of the inhabitants and the fear of their foes, the Turks, and save for an occasional expedition against the brigands or friction with the fiscal officials, his time passed peaceably and pleasantly. But in 1811 he was recalled to Paris to receive orders before starting on a new sphere of duty.

Masséna, "the spoiled child of victory," had met his match at Torres Vedras, and Napoleon, blaming the man instead of the system, had determined to try a fresh leader for the army opposing Sir Arthur Wellesley. The emperor did not hide from himself the fact that in selecting Marmont he was making an experiment, for he told St. Cyr that he had sent Marmont to Spain because he had plenty of talent, but that he had not yet tested to the full his force of character, and he added, "I shall soon be able to judge of that, for now he is left to his own resources."

The new commander of the Army of Portugal set out with the full confidence that the task was not beyond his powers, and with the promise of the viceroyalty of one of the five provinces into which Spain was to be divided. He arrived at the front two days after the battle of Fuentes d'Onoro, and found a very different state of affairs from what he had expected. The country was a howling waste covered with fierce guerrillas. The French army, so long accustomed to success, was absolutely demoralised by repeated disappointments and defeats. It was necessary to take stringent measures to restore the morale of the troops before he could call on them to face once more "the infantry whose fire was the most murderous of all the armies of Europe."

Accordingly he withdrew from the Portuguese frontier, put his army into cantonments round Salamanca, and set to work on the difficult task of collecting supplies from a country which was already swept bare. Meanwhile he split up his army into six divisions, established direct communications between himself and the divisional officers, and, to get rid of the grumblers, gave leave to all officers, who so desired, to return to France. At the same time he distributed his weak battalions among the other corps so that each battalion had a complement of seven hundred muskets. He also broke up the weak squadrons and batteries and brought up the remainder to service strength. Scarcely was this reorganisation completed when Soult, who had been defeated at Albuera, called on Marmont to aid him in saving Badajoz. In spite of his personal dislike for the Duke of Dalmatia, the marshal hurried to his aid and for the time the important fortress was saved. During the rest of the summer the Army of Portugal lay in the valley of the Tagus, holding the bridge of Almaraz, and thus ready at any moment to go to the relief of Badajoz or Ciudad Rodrigo, the two keys of Portugal. When, in the autumn, Wellington threatened Ciudad Rodrigo, the marshal, calling to his aid Dorsenne, who commanded in Northern Spain, at the successful engagement of El Bodin drove back the advance guard of the Anglo-Portuguese and threw a large quantity of provisions into the fortress.

The year 1812 was a disastrous one for the French arms all over Europe. The emperor attempted to direct the Spanish War from Paris. In his desire to secure all Southern Spain, he stripped Marmont's army to reinforce Suchet in his conquest of Valencia. Accordingly in January the marshal was powerless to stop Wellington's dash at Ciudad Rodrigo, and was unable later to make a sufficient demonstration in Portugal to relieve the pressure on Badajoz; so both the fortresses fell, and the Duke of Ragusa was blamed for the emperor's mistake. He was thereafter called upon to try to stem the victorious advance of the English into Spain. Short of men, of horses, and of supplies, he did wonders. Thanks to his strenuous efforts, supplies were massed at Salamanca, good food and careful nursing emptied the hospitals and filled the ranks, and the cavalry was supplied with remounts by dismounting the "field officers" of the infantry.

The month of July saw an interesting duel round Salamanca between Marmont and Wellington. The two armies were very nearly equal in numbers, the French having forty-seven thousand men and the English forty-four thousand. The French had the advantage of a broad base with lines of retreat either on Burgos or Madrid. The English had to cover their single line of communication, which ran through Ciudad Rodrigo. The French had the further advantage that their infantry marched better than the English.

Owing to these causes their commander was so far able to out-general his adversary that by July 22nd he was actually threatening the English line of retreat. But a tactical mistake threw away all these strategic advantages. In his eagerness he allowed his leading division to get too extended, forgetting that he was performing the dangerous operation of a flank march. Wellington waited till he saw his opportunity and then threw himself on the weak French centre and cut the French army in half, thus proving his famous dictum that the great general is not he who makes fewest mistakes, but he who can best take advantage of the mistakes of his enemy. Marmont saw his error as soon as the English attack began, but a wound from a cannon ball disabled him at the very commencement of the action. This injury to his arm was so serious that he had to throw up his command and return to France, and for the whole of the next year he had to wear his arm in a sling.

Napoleon, furious with the marshal for his ill-success, most unjustly blamed him for not waiting for reinforcements: these actually arrived two days after the battle. Joseph, however, had told him distinctly that he was not going to send him any help, and if it had not been for his tactical blunders, Marmont would undoubtedly have caused Wellington to fall back on Portugal. But in 1812 the exigencies of war demanded that France should send forth every soldier, and accordingly in March the Duke of Ragusa was gazetted to the command of the sixth corps, which was forming in the valley of the Maine. On taking up this command he found that his corps was mainly composed of sailors drafted from the useless ships, and of recruits, while his artillery had no horses and his cavalry did not exist. With these raw troops he had to undergo some difficult experiences at Lützen and Bautzen, but, as the campaign progressed, he moulded them into shape, and his divisions did good service in the fighting in Silesia and round Dresden. At the rout after the battle of Leipzig, Marmont, like most of the higher officers of the army, thought more of his personal safety than of his honour, and allowed himself to be escorted from the field by his staff officers.

But in the campaign of 1814 he made amends for all his former blunders, and his fighting record stands high indeed. At Saint-Dizier, La Rothière, Arcis-sur-Aube, Nogent, Sézanne, and Champaubert, he held his own or defeated the enemy with inferior numbers in every case. Once only at Laon did he allow himself to be surprised. When the end came it was Marmont who, at Joseph's command, had to hand over Paris to the Allies. Thereafter he was faced with a terrible problem. His army was sick of fighting, officers and men demanded peace. He had to decide whether his duty to Napoleon was the same as his duty to France. Unfortunately he acted hurriedly, and, without informing the emperor, entered into negotiations with the enemy.

The result was far-reaching, for his conduct showed Alexander that the army was sick of war and would no longer fight for Napoleon. It thus cut away the ground of the commissioners who were trying, by trading on the prestige of the emperor and the fear of his name, to persuade the Czar to accept Napoleon's abdication on behalf of his son, the king of Rome. The marshal's enemies put down his action to ill-will against the emperor for withholding for so long the marshalate and for his treatment after Salamanca. But Marmont asserted that it was patriotism which dictated his action, and further maintained that Napoleon himself ought to have approved of his action, quoting a conversation held in 1813. "If the enemy invaded France," said the emperor, "and seized the heights of Montmartre, you would naturally believe that the safety of your country would command you to leave me, and if you did so you would be a good Frenchman, a brave man, a conscientious man, but not a man of honour."

The defection of the Duke of Ragusa came as a bitter blow to Napoleon. "That Marmont should do such a thing," cried the fallen emperor, "a man with whom I have shared my bread, whom I drew out of obscurity! Ungrateful villain, he will be more unhappy than I."

The prophecy was true. The Duke of Ragusa stuck to the Bourbons and refused to join Napoleon during the Hundred Days, going to Ghent as chief of the military household of the exiled king. He returned with Louis to Paris, and was made major-general of the Royal Guard and a peer of France, in which capacity he sat as one of the judges who condemned Ney to death. But men looked askance at him, and from 1817 he lived in retirement, occupying his leisure in experimental farming, with great injury to his purse, for his elaborate scheme of housing his sheep in three-storied barns and clothing them in coats made of skin was most unprofitable. Retirement was a bitter blow to the keen soldier, but the Bourbon monarchs clearly understood that the deserter of Napoleon and the judge of Marshal Ney could never be popular with the army.

Still, when in July, 1830, discontent was seething, Charles X. remembered his sterling qualities and summoned him to Paris as governor of the city. It was an unfortunate nomination, for the marshal's unpopularity weakened the bonds of discipline, whilst his eagerness to show his loyalty caused him to adopt such measures as the king ordered, irrespective of their military worth. In vain he warned the king that this was not a revolt but a revolution; the counsels of Polignac were all powerful. The marshal's political suggestions were unheeded and his military plans overridden. The mass of the troops of the line, kept for long hours without food in the streets, mutinied and went over to the populace, while those who remained loyal, and the royal guards, instead of being concentrated and protected by batteries of artillery, were frittered away in useless expeditions into outlying parts of the city. After two days' fighting the royalists had to evacuate the city. Thus it fell to the lot of the marshal once more to hand over Paris to the foes of those to whom his allegiance was due.

The Duke of Ragusa accompanied Charles to Cherbourg and quitted France in August, 1830, never to return. The remainder of his life was spent in foreign countries. He made Vienna his headquarters, and from there took journeys to Russia, Turkey, Egypt, and Italy. Deeply interested in science and history, he devoted his leisure to writing his *Memoirs*, to works on military science, philanthropy, and travel. Thus occupied, though an exile from his country, he lived a busy, active, and on the whole useful life till death overtook him at Vienna in 1852.

Marshal Marmont has been called one of Napoleon's failures, but this criticism is one-sided and unjust. True it is that his name is intimately connected with the failure in Spain and with the fall of the Empire, but to judge his career by these two instances and to neglect his other work, is to generalise from an insufficient and casual basis. The Duke of Ragusa owed his marshalate, like many others, to his intimacy with Napoleon, but unlike several of the marshals he really earned his baton. His great powers of organisation, so unstintedly given to the re-armament of France and Italy, and his work of regeneration in Dalmatia, together with his military operations in Styria, Spain, and during the campaign of 1814, mark him out as a soldier of great capabilities. Organisation was his strong point, but he also possessed great physical bravery and many of the qualities of a commander.

His love for his profession was great, and not only had he graduated under Napoleon's eye, but much of his time was spent in studying his calling from a scientific and historical point of view. As a strategist he probably stood as high as any of his fellow Marshals, and his operations in Dalmatia, Spain, and France deserve the careful study of all students of military history. But he failed as a tactician. Salamanca and Laon prove not only that he made mistakes and had not the faculty of retrieving his errors, but above all he lacked the capacity of seizing on the mistakes of his enemy.

In 1811 at El Bodin he had Wellington at his mercy, but he hesitated to strike, for he could not believe his great opponent could make the glaring error of leaving his divisions unsupported. Again and again during his career he showed that lack of resolution which was responsible for his last catastrophe in Paris, where he allowed his own judgment to be overruled by King Charles's personal desires. In a word, he had the gift of a great quartermaster-general rather than of a commander-in-chief. As a man the marshal's character is an interesting study. In youth the thirst for personal glory and ambition were the dominant traits, and what stability he had he drew from his proud sense of honour, which refused to allow him to take plunder or bribes. But responsibility developed many latent qualities. The desire to keep his troops efficient led him to pay especial care to their physical well-being, and from doing this as a duty he learned to do it as a labour of love.

As time went on, desire for personal glory became merged in keen delight in the glory of France, and hence grew up a patriotism which rightly or wrongly led to the scenes of 1814 and 1830. Misfortune also had its share in the enlarging of his character. His unhappy marriage, his bitterness at the withholding of the marshalate, his unpopularity after 1814, led him to remember his father's warning that success is not everything, and turned his attention to the development of those scientific and literary abilities to which he had always shown strong leanings. Hence, though the blight of his marriage and his unpopularity, arising from his desertion of Napoleon, embittered him and caused his *Memoirs* to teem with cutting descriptions of his contemporaries and former friends, his old age, though spent in exile, was soothed by congenial work which proved "that to the eye of a general he united the accomplishments of a scholar and the heart of a philanthropist."